GW00374528

SCHOLAR Study Guide

CfE Advanced Higher Economics

Unit 2: National and global economic issues

and

Unit 3: Researching an economic issue

Authored by:

Colin Spence (Culloden Academy)

Reviewed by:

Wilson Turkington (Edinburgh Academy)

Heriot-Watt University

Edinburgh EH14 4AS, United Kingdom.

Copyright Page

First published 2016 by Heriot-Watt University.

This edition published in 2016 by Heriot-Watt University SCHOLAR.

Copyright © 2016 SCHOLAR Forum.

Distributed by the SCHOLAR Forum.

SCHOLAR Study Guide Unit 2 and Unit 3: CfE Advanced Higher Economics

1. CfE Advanced Higher Economics Course Code: C722 77

ISBN 978-1-911057-13-0

Print Production and fulfilment in UK by Print Trail www.printtrail.com

Acknowledgements

Thanks are due to the members of Heriot-Watt University's SCHOLAR team who planned and created these materials, and to the many colleagues who reviewed the content.

We would like to acknowledge the assistance of the education authorities, colleges, teachers and students who contributed to the SCHOLAR programme and who evaluated these materials.

Grateful acknowledgement is made for permission to use the following material in the SCHOLAR programme:

The Scottish Qualifications Authority for permission to use Past Papers assessments.

The Scottish Government for financial support.

The content of this Study Guide is aligned to the Scottish Qualifications Authority (SQA) curriculum.

Contents

Topic 1

Recent trends in the national economy (Unit 2)

Contents

Prerequisite knowledge

This topic assumes no previous knowledge and is intended to be accessible for those studying Economics for the first time. However, if you have already completed Higher Economics you will be familiar with some of the concepts outlined.

Learning objectives

By the end of this topic you should be able to evaluate recent economic trends in the national economy by:

- *describing recent trends in economic indicators;*

- *explaining reasons for a recent trend in an economic indicator;*

- *update all data with the latest information from respected sources.*

This topic includes the latest economic trends at the time this note was produced. You will be asked to update these details and compose your own updated notes. Potential sources include the BBC, ONS, Guardian and Telegraph websites.

1.1   Gross domestic product (GDP)

The UK's economy grew by 2.6% in 2014. In 2013 the economy grew by 1.7%.

ONS figures showed the economy grew by 0.6% in the final three months of 2014, a slowdown from 0.7% growth recorded in the previous quarter.

The main points from the ONS report issued on 28 April 2015 are:

- Change in gross domestic product (GDP) is the main indicator of economic growth. GDP is estimated to have increased by 0.3% in Quarter 1 (Jan to Mar) 2015 compared with growth of 0.6% in Quarter 4 (Oct to Dec) 2014.

- Output increased in services by 0.5% in Quarter 1 2015. The other three main industrial groupings within the economy decreased, with construction falling by 1.6%, production by 0.1% and agriculture by 0.2%.

- GDP was 2.4% higher in Quarter 1 2015 compared with the same quarter a year ago.

- In Quarter 1 2015, GDP was estimated to have been 4.0% higher than the pre-economic downturn peak of Quarter 1 2008. From the peak in Quarter 1 2008 to the trough in Quarter 2 (Apr to June) 2009, the economy shrank by 6.0%.

Note that early ONS figures are prone to revision as more data comes in, although the changes are generally minor.

GDP

Go online

Q1:   Locate the latest figures for the UK's gross domestic product and add them to your notes.

. . . .

Q2:   Locate two up-to-date articles, giving the main points regarding the recent progress of GDP. You may wish to retain these on a memory stick.

. . . .

Suggested online sources: BBC, ONS, The Guardian, The Telegraph.

. . . .

1.2   Inflation

Early in 2015, the rate of inflation turned negative (i.e. deflation), although both the Chancellor of the Exchequer and the Governor of the Bank of England stated that they did not expect this to continue for long.

In May 2015, the ONS drew attention to the following main points:

- The Consumer Prices Index (CPI) fell by 0.1% in the year to April 2015, compared to no change (0.0%) in the year to March 2015.

- This is the first time the CPI has fallen over the year since official records began in 1996 and the first time since 1960 based on comparable historic estimates.

- The largest downward contribution came from transport services - notably air and sea fares, with the timing of Easter this year a likely factor.

Inflation

Q3:   Locate the latest figures for the UK's inflation rate and add them to your notes.

. . . .

Go online

Q4:   Locate two up-to-date articles, giving the main points regarding the recent progress of inflation. You may wish to retain these on a memory stick.

. . . .

Suggested online sources: BBC, ONS, The Guardian, The Telegraph.

. . . .

1.3   Unemployment

In May 2015, the ONS drew attention to the following main points:

- Comparing the estimates for January to March 2015 with those for October to December 2014, employment continued to rise and unemployment continued to fall. These changes maintain the general direction of movement since late 2011 to early 2012.

- There were 31.1 million people in work, 202,000 more than for October to December 2014 and 564,000 more than for a year earlier.

- The proportion of people aged from 16 to 64 in work (the employment rate) was 73.5%, the highest since comparable records began in 1971.

- There were 1.83 million unemployed people. This was 35,000 fewer than for October to December 2014, the smallest quarterly fall since June to August 2013. Comparing January to March 2015 with a year earlier, there were 386,000 fewer unemployed people.

- The proportion of the economically active population who were unemployed (the unemployment rate) was 5.5%, lower than for October to December 2014 (5.7%)

and for a year earlier (6.8%). The economically active population is those in work plus those seeking and available to work.

- There were 8.98 million people aged from 16 to 64 who were out of work and not seeking or available to work (known as **economically inactive**), 69,000 fewer than for October to December 2014 but little changed compared with a year earlier.

- The proportion of people aged from 16 to 64 who were economically inactive (the inactivity rate) was 22.1%, lower than for October to December 2014 (22.3%) but unchanged compared with a year earlier.

- Comparing January to March 2015 with a year earlier, pay for employees in Great Britain increased by 1.9% including bonuses and by 2.2% excluding bonuses.

A number of graphs sourced from the ONS are available, should you wish extra detail on employment trends.

Unemployment trends

Go online

Use your knowledge of economics and current affairs to comment on the possible reasons for the trends in each graph below. Discuss these with your teacher/tutor.

Q5: Jobless totals:

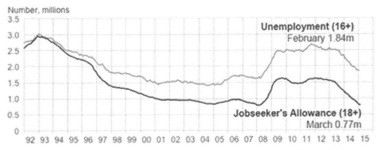

Jobless total: Unemployment and Jobseeker's Allowance in the UK 1992-2015
Source: ONS (Office of National Statistics)

. . . .

Q6: Employment rates:

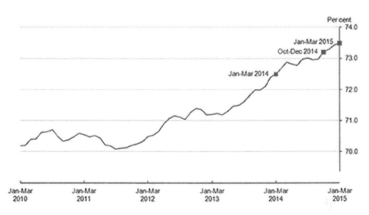

Employment rate (aged 16-64), **seasonally adjusted**
Source: ONS

. . . .

Q7: Public sector employment:

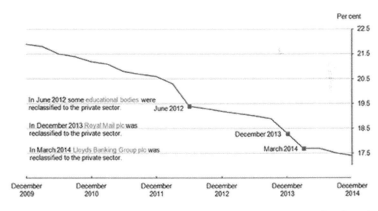

Public sector employment as a percentage of total employment, seasonally adjusted
Source: ONS

. . . .

Q8: Earnings and price growth:

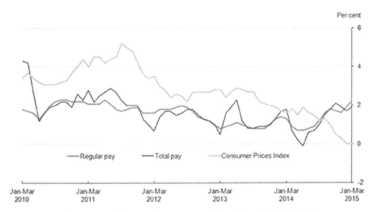

Average earnings and consumer prices annual growth rates
Source: ONS

. . . .

Q9: Economic inactivity rate:

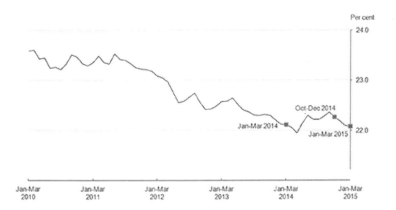

Economic inactivity rate (aged 16 to 64), seasonally adjusted
Source: ONS

. . . .

Q10: Locate the latest figures for the UK's unemployment and add them to your notes.

. . . .

Q11: Locate two up-to-date articles, giving the main points regarding the most recent changes in unemployment. You may wish to retain these on a memory stick.

....

Suggested online sources: BBC, ONS, The Guardian, The Telegraph.

....

1.4 The budget deficit

The deficit forecast to be 6.6% of GDP this year, 5.5% in 2014-15 then falling to 0.8% by 2017-18 with a surplus of 0.2% in 2018-19.

The government has not met their targets in this area in recent years, so it is likely that these forecasts will change.

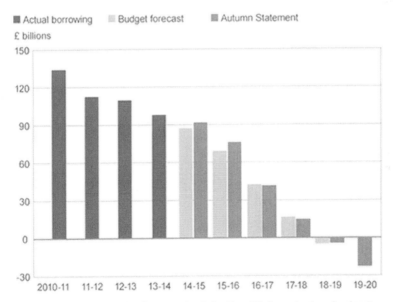

UK Government borrowing forecasts (excludes Royal Mail pension transfer, Asset Purchase Facility and public sector banks)
Source: ONS and OBR (Office for Budget Responsibility)

Borrowing was £108bn last year and is forecast to be under £90bn this year, leading to a surplus of almost £5bn in 2018-19.

The budget deficit

Q12: How desirable is a balanced budget?

Go online

....

1.5   The exchange rate

The recent trend illustrated in the graphs below has been for the pound to weaken against the dollar, but to strengthen against the euro.

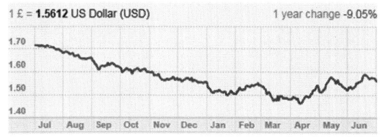

Exchange rate between UK pound sterling and US dollar
Source: The Financial Times (http://www.ft.com/markets)

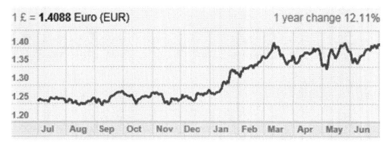

Exchange rate between UK pound sterling and the euro
Source: The Financial Times (http://www.ft.com/markets)

The exchange rate

Q13: Which of the three currencies has been strongest over the 12 months to May 2015?

Go online

....

Q14: Locate the latest figures for the exchange rate of the pound to both the dollar and the euro. Add them to your notes.

....

Q15: Locate two up-to-date articles, giving the main points regarding the most recent changes in exchange rates. You may wish to retain these on a memory stick.

....

Suggested online sources: BBC.

....

1.6 The balance of payments

ONS reported that:

- **Seasonally adjusted**, the UK's deficit on trade in goods and services was estimated to have been £2.8 billion in March 2015, compared with £3.3 billion in February 2015.

- This reflects a deficit of £10.1 billion on goods, partially offset by an estimated surplus of £7.3 billion on services.

- In Quarter 1 (Jan to Mar) 2015, the UK's deficit on trade in goods and services was estimated to have been £7.5 billion; widening by £1.5 billion from the previous quarter.

- In Quarter 1 2015, the trade in goods deficit widened by £0.8 billion to £29.9 billion. The widening reflects a £2.7 billion fall in exports and a £1.9 billion fall in imports.

- At the commodity level, the fall in exports in quarter 1 reflects a £2.2 billion decrease in exports of fuels; specifically, oil exported to EU countries, which fell by £2.1 billion from the previous quarter. Over the same period, imports of fuels fell by £2.2 billion, reflecting a £1.8 billion fall in imports of oil from outside the EU.

The balance of payments

Q16: Comment on the possible causes of fall in exports of goods from January to March.

Go online

....

Q17: Locate the latest figures for the UK's balance of payments and add them to your notes.

....

Q18: Locate two up-to-date articles, giving the main points regarding the most recent changes in the balance of payments. You may wish to retain these on a memory stick.

....

Suggested online sources: BBC, ONS, The Guardian, The Telegraph.

....

1.7   House prices

UK house prices accelerated with a 9.6% increase in the year to the end of March 2015, according to official figures.

A lack in the supply of homes on the market is thought to be behind the increase. The annual rate of increase accelerated from 7.4% a month earlier. In Scotland prices rose at 14.6%, the fastest since 2007. This was above the UK average.

The Land and Buildings Transaction Tax replaced UK stamp duty land tax in Scotland from 1 April, which "may have had an impact" on the increase in prices, according to the Office for National Statistics (ONS).

There were also double-digit percentage annual property price rises in the East of England (11.4%), London (11.2%) and the South East of England (11.2%), the ONS figures also show.

The ONS said that the cost of the average UK home in March was over £270,000, ranging from £498,000 in London to £145,000 in Northern Ireland (source: BBC website - http://bbc.in/1lih87g).

Go online

House prices

Q19: Locate the latest figures for the UK's house prices and add them to your notes.

....

Q20: Locate two up-to-date articles, giving the main points regarding the most recent changes in house prices. You may wish to retain these on a memory stick.

....

Suggested online sources: BBC, ONS, The Guardian, The Telegraph.

....

1.8   Oil prices

Oil comes in various types and qualities. As a benchmark for the prices of North Sea oil, that from the Brent field is typically quoted. The **spot market** is the price for immediate delivery, and can be slightly different from prices quoted on the **futures market** where contracts are for forward delivery. The diagram below shows that the spot price fell rapidly in late 2014.

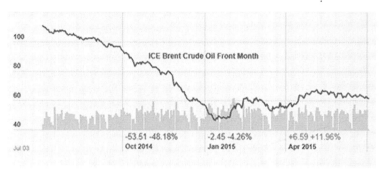

Brent crude oil spot price ($/barrel)
Source: The Financial Times (http://www.ft.com/markets)

Oil prices

Q21: Oil prices depend on supply and demand. Suggest some factors that could contribute to changes in the oil price.

Go online

....

Q22: Locate the latest figures for the oil prices (Brent Crude) and add them to your notes.

....

Q23: Locate two up-to-date articles, giving the main points regarding the most recent changes in oil prices. You may wish to retain these on a memory stick.

....

Suggested online sources: BBC, ONS, The Guardian, The Telegraph.

1.9   Summary

┌─ Summary ───

You should now be able to evaluate recent economic trends in the national economy by:

- describing recent trends in economic indicators;

- explaining reasons for a recent trend in an economic indicator;

- update all data with the latest information from respected sources.

Topic 2

Controlling the budget deficit and the national debt (Unit 2)

Contents

Prerequisite knowledge

This topic assumes no previous knowledge and is intended to be accessible for those studying Economics for the first time. However if you have already completed Higher Economics you will be familiar with some of the concepts outlined.

Learning objectives

By the end of this topic you should be able to:

- *explain reasons why we have a budget deficit;*

- *explain the significance of the UK national debt;*

- *explain recent trends in the budget deficit;*

- *evaluate the effectiveness of recent government policy in reducing the budget deficit;*

- *update all data with the latest information from respected sources.*

2.1   What makes this an important UK economic issue

One of the most significant issues affecting the UK economy is the size of the national debt, and the related issue of controlling the annual budget deficits which add to it. It has become a primary concern for UK governments and to date the attempts to reduce the deficit and the national debt have had mixed or even disappointing outcomes. It impacts on fiscal policy and through this on living standards and economic growth. This looks like continuing to be an issue for some years ahead.

This section illustrates some of the data and information that your research should reveal. If you are considering a dissertation in this area, you will need to update all the data that follows. Therefore, the major activity to be carried out throughout this topic is to obtain the latest figures.

2.2   Why the UK has a budget deficit

The UK has a budget deficit for the following reasons:

- **Fiscal policy** - the UK Government in the majority of years has public spending levels that exceed its tax revenues;

- **The structural deficit** - the UK Government makes major infrastructure investments which, although beneficial to the economy in the long term, add to the borrowing requirement. This **structural deficit** continues even when the economy is expanding;

- **Recession** - during recessions, UK Government spending in areas such as welfare increases but at the same time tax revenues reduce because personal and corporate incomes fall;

- **Interest payments** - maintaining the debt requires the payment of interest every year and this places further pressure on government spending. Higher bond yields will cause interest payments to increase.

Budget deficit reasons

Go online

Match the reason for a budget deficit with the statements in the following questions.

Q1:   A decline in economic activity reduces tax revenues.

a) Fiscal policy
b) The structural deficit
c) Recession
d) Interest payments

. . . .

Q2: Borrowing for major infrastructure investment.

a) Fiscal policy
b) The structural deficit
c) Recession
d) Interest payments

....

Q3: Government spends more than it raises.

a) Fiscal policy
b) The structural deficit
c) Recession
d) Interest payments

....

Q4: The cost of funding the national debt curbs spending.

a) Fiscal policy
b) The structural deficit
c) Recession
d) Interest payments

....

2.2.1 Why 2009/10 was the peak year for borrowing

Public sector borrowing peaked in 2009/10 at £167.4bn. Factors that contributed to this exceptional year included:

- the economic crisis that followed the "credit crunch" resulted in reduced incomes and hence reduced income tax receipts;

- a cut in the rate of VAT which was a fiscal measure aimed at increasing aggregate demand and stimulating the economy but in the short term reduced tax revenues.

- higher benefits were paid due to higher unemployment in recession;

- Government spending on areas such as the NHS had increased significantly over the decade.

Government borrowing

Q5: Why does government have to borrow?

....

Go online

2.2.2 The issue of asset sales from the public sector

Note that the government can make asset sales from the public sector and this is regarded as reducing the annual deficit. Therefore the privatisation of Royal Mail contributed to a reduction in that year's deficit. Funds from the sale of the assets are further increased by the receipt of the Royal Mail pension fund.

The government had to adopt the pension fund liabilities of the Royal Mail to make the sale attractive to the private investors. These pension fund liabilities will run forward for decades and add to public spending and hence the deficit. In other words, an apparent reduction in one year's deficit could turn out to have a negative impact on the deficit overall in the long term.

Sale of public sector assets

Go online

Q6:   What is questionable about treating the sale of public sector assets as income for one year?

. . . .

2.3   The extent of UK national debt and how it compares with other countries

The national debt is the accumulation of government borrowing over centuries. Every year in which there is a budget deficit adds to it. The government has to pay interest on this debt to finance it and this varies with interest rates but typically will be tens of billions of pounds. In order to reduce the national debt the government would need to have a budget surplus.

It should also be recognised that the UK national debt:

- is currently financed at low rates of interest;

- has repayment dates that are more spread out over the medium and long term than those of many other countries;

- is to an extent owed to others within the UK economy such as pension funds and individuals (and this portion is a transfer of income from taxpayers to savers and does not leave the UK economy).

In 2015, the government considers control of the budget deficit as an economic priority. The chancellor (George Osborne) announced that the Committee of the Commissioners for the Reduction of the National Debt would meet for the first time in more than 150 years. This group which includes the governor of the Bank of England last met in the aftermath of the Napoleonic Wars to address the issue of national debt.

The following map shows a comparison of the gross debt of the 28 European Union member states as a percentage of GDP (figures from 2013).

The absolute value of the national debt is not helpful for international or historic comparisons. Everything is relative, and for this topic the key measure is the national debt compared to annual GDP. This shows the significance of the debt by comparing it to the overall annual output of a nation's economy. The map below follows and illustrates this point.

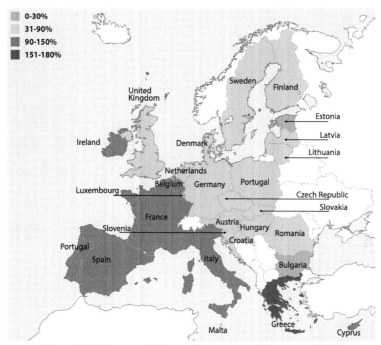

Gross debt of European Union member states as a percentage of GDP

National debt comparison

Q7: Name the European Union member countries that have a greater problem with their accumulated national debt than the UK.

Go online

The column chart that follows will help you to confirm your answer.

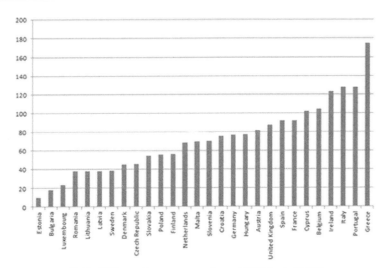

Debt of EU countries as a percentage of GDP (end of 2013)

. . . .

Q8:   Carry out some research and establish the debt to GDP ratios of:

a) USA;
b) Japan;
c) Australia.

. . . .

Q9:   Research the most recent figures available for the debt of EU countries.

. . . .

Q10: Find a UK national debt calculator online. You could note down the current figure, but it will change as you look at it! You may also find a calculator for the US debt.

. . . .

2.4   How the current UK deficit compares with historic levels

The diagram below shows net UK Government borrowing and indicates the dramatic increase in the UK deficit in recent years.

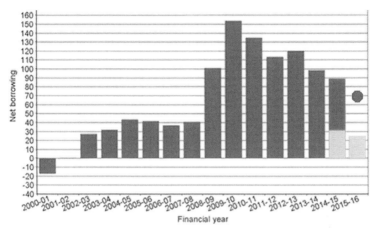

Financial year

UK public sector borrowing from 2001 to 2016 (forecast)
(Source: ONS (http://bit.ly/1FjSLpd))

Net borrowing year to date for 2014-15 and 2015-16 is shown in light blue. The dark blue dot indicates the full financial year forecast for 2015-16.

Recent trends in UK government borrowing

Q11: Describe recent trends in UK government borrowing.

....

Go online

The comparison of UK net borrowing to the GDP is a useful way of looking at the relative size of the budget deficit. The years ahead are forecasts and going on the failure of previous predictions, may not turn out as expected.

The bar graph below shows the UK net borrowing as a percentage of GDP using figures from the Office of National Statistics. The bars showing light blue denote the forecast figures (future predictions).

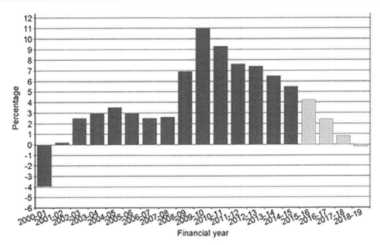

Financial year

UK net borrowing as a percentage of GDP

Budget deficit forecast figures

Q12: Research the most recent figures and observe how they compare to the forecast
figures.

Go online

....

2.5   The effectiveness of recent government policy in reducing the budget deficit

The latest figures available, at the time of writing, show that **public sector net
borrowing (PSNB)** was £86.3bn from April to December 2014. This is only 0.1% lower
than the same period in 2013. During the same period the national debt increased
significantly.

The newly elected government of 2015 has put forward the following proposal on the
topic of budget deficits.

The Chancellor of the Exchequer, George Osborne, said,

"In normal times, governments of the left as well as the right should run a budget
surplus to bear down on debt and prepare for an uncertain future".

This is a pledge to balance the public sector books but of course it remains at the whim
of a future government to change this approach.

Given how tightly public spending has already been squeezed over the years 2010-
2015, it will be very difficult and probably not desirable to reduce it as rapidly as the
Chancellor has indicated.   The level of debt has continued to increase despite the
reductions in public spending and many view the policy of austerity as having failed

(see article below).

As a student of Economics you should research and form your own view on the efficacy of the government policy. The opposition statements below should not be treated uncritically.

The extract below is from the Sunday Herald (5 July 2015) where the SNP's John Swinney presents the opinion under the headline 'The cuts don't work... stop them'.

"The experiment in austerity has been a failure by any benchmark. GDP per capita - a key measure of our economic strength - is forecast to take two years longer to return to pre-recession levels than it did following the Great Depression of the 1930s.

Austerity has even failed in its principal objective of cutting the deficit. Over the six years to 2016, the Chancellor is likely to miss the borrowing targets he set for himself when he first entered office in 2010 by a staggering £150 billion. It's simple economics that a programme of austerity and cuts that reduces household income and damages economic confidence weakens rather than strengthens the public finances."

The Labour Party's spokesperson said,

"The figures show George Osborne has broken his promise to balance the books by this year and national debt is still rising."

"His failure on the deficit is because falling living standards over the last five years have led to tax revenues falling short. This government is now set to have borrowed over £200bn more than planned."

Reliability of sources

Q13: Consider the reliability of the opposition sources quoted above.

. . . .

Go online

2.6   Summary

> **Summary**
>
> You should now be able to:
>
> * explain reasons why we have a budget deficit;
>
> * explain the significance of the UK national debt;
>
> * explain recent trends in the budget deficit;
>
> * evaluate the effectiveness of recent government policy in reducing the budget deficit;
>
> * update all data with the latest information from respected sources.

2.7 End of topic test

End of Topic 2 test

Go online

Q14: Which of these does **not** cause the annual budget deficit to increase?

a) Higher interest charges on the national debt
b) Higher rates of economic growth
c) Increased infrastructure spending by government
d) Reductions in VAT receipts

. . . .

Q15: UK net borrowing as a percent of GDP peaked in:

a) 2008-09
b) 2009-10
c) 2010-11
d) 2011-12

. . . .

Q16: The structural deficit exists because of:

a) increased benefit spending during recession.
b) reduced income tax receipts during recession.
c) long-term investment in infrastructure by government.
d) the privatisation of public sector assets.

. . . .

Q17: Government policies from 2010-1015 that have been described as "austerity" have by the end of that period:

a) led to a reduction in the national debt.
b) produced a shorter downturn than the great depression of the 1930s.
c) have left the UK with one of the smallest borrowing to GDP percentages in the EU.
d) led to falls in UK net borrowing as a percentage of GDP.

. . . .

Topic 3

Trends in the Scottish oil industry (Unit 2)

Contents

Prerequisite knowledge

This topic assumes no previous knowledge and is intended to be accessible for those studying Economics for the first time. However if you have already completed Higher Economics you will be familiar with some of the concepts outlined.

Learning objectives

By the end of this topic you should be able to:

- *describe recent economic trends in the oil industry;*

- *explain oil price fluctuations;*

- *evaluate the impact of oil price changes on the Scottish economy;*

- *update all data with the latest information from respected sources.*

3.1   Production trends in the North Sea oil industry

This topic examines the latest economic trends in the oil industry at the time of publishing. You will be asked to update these details and compose your own updated notes. This will provide you with the latest information.

Your main sources could be the BBC and ONS websites. Alternatively you may search for alternative articles - The Guardian and The Telegraph websites are two possible sources of relevant articles. The Aberdeen-based regional daily The Press and Journal will also contain many oil-related articles.

Some of these newspaper articles are written against the background of Scottish politics and contain a significant political bias so should be handled with care.

3.2   Falling UK oil production

Using the expected boundary line in the North Sea between Scotland and the rest of the UK, more than 95% of oil production would have been in the Scottish sector in recent years. (50-60% of current UK gas production is also produced in the Scottish sector.)

Exploration effort has decreased but demand for licenses is high.

Interest in the North Sea remains high with 410 blocks licensed in the 27th round. This is an all-time high.

Licensing round

Q1:   The figure for the 28th licensing round was published in the week this topic was

Go online   prepared. Find out how many blocks were awarded in this round and any subsequent licensing rounds. Read any accompanying article(s).

. . . .

Production to present: 42 billion barrels.

Remaining North Sea oil has been estimated to be in the range of 15-24 billion barrels. (Source: Oil and Gas UK)

The Department of Energy & Climate Change (DECC) estimate predicts 11-21 billion barrels. The DECC has also produced a very cautious prediction of 10.4 billion barrels produced by 2050.

Reliability of sources

Q2:   Consider the reliability of the following sources (referred to above):

Go online

    a) Oil and Gas UK;

    b) The Department of Energy and Climate Change.

. . . .

Here is a summary taken from a report on the BBC website dated 28 July 2015 that refers to the quarterly output in the oil and gas sector.

"UK economic growth accelerated in the second quarter of the year, helped by a big jump in oil and gas production, official figures have shown.

The ONS said manufacturing output experienced its first fall in two years with output dropping 0.3% in the quarter. However, a surge in North Sea oil and gas production lifted overall industrial output by 1% - the biggest increase since late 2010. The "mining and quarrying" component of the industrial output figures, which includes oil and gas extraction, rose by 7.8% in the quarter, the biggest increase since 1989.

The ONS said the increase, which came despite falling oil prices, was driven by tax cuts in March designed to support the sector."

Quarterly output in the oil and gas sector

Q3: Locate this article and an up-to-date equivalent. With these quarterly figures being regularly announced by the ONS, the information will be available on a range of news, business or economics websites. How has the situation altered since 2015?

Go online

....

3.3   Oil price trends and predictions

As with predicted production, there are different views on the direction of future oil prices in the medium term.

The Office of Budget Responsibility (OBR) predict that prices will fall. The International Energy Agency, Department of Energy and Climate Change and US Department of Energy believe that prices will rise.

Given this divergence of opinion among specialised agencies, you with your knowledge of Economics, should feel capable of making your own mind up - either way, you won't be without support.

Oil price predictions may influence the UK constitutional debate on Scotland. This is because oil revenues would be a significant contribution to the GDP and public finances of an independent Scotland.

The diagram below shows the price of Brent Crude (the North Sea benchmark for oil prices) on the first of every month since 1 September 2013 in US dollars.

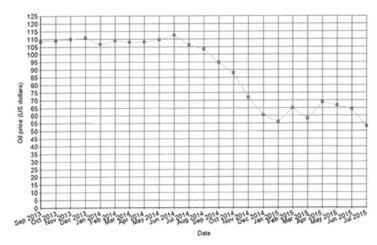

Brent Crude oil prices (in US dollars) from 2013 to 2015

Brent Crude

Q4: Find out the latest price for Brent Crude.

Go online

. . . .

3.4   Causes of oil price fluctuations

Oil prices fluctuate in a global market and as with any market, the interaction of supply and demand causes the price to move.

In June 2014, the price of Brent crude was up around $115 per barrel which highlights the significant drop in prices, so why have they fallen?

Demand factors

Demand for energy is closely related to economic activity. For the majority of the past decade, oil prices have been high, often above $100 per barrel. Soaring oil consumption in countries like China meant that oil production in conventional fields couldn't keep up with demand, so prices rose.

From Autumn 2014, demand for oil in places like Europe, Asia, and the USA began tapering off, due to weakening economies and new efficiency measures.

Demand is low because of lower economic growth in China, continuing problems in the Eurozone, increased efficiency, and a growing switch away from oil to other fuels. For example, vehicles are becoming more energy-efficient. Even the seasons and the weather play a part as demand increases in the winter in the northern hemisphere.

Supply factors

High prices had encouraged companies in the USA and Canada to start drilling for new, hard-to-extract crude in North Dakota's shale formations and Alberta's oil sands. By the end of 2014, world oil supply was on track to rise beyond actual demand, so the unused oil was simply stored for later. Storage space is limited and so purchases of oil (demand) fell, causing a decrease in prices.

Supply can also be affected by weather such as hurricanes in the Gulf of Mexico, and by political instability in oil-producing regions such as Iraq and Libya. Price expectations have an important effect. If producers think the price is staying high, they invest, which after a lag boosts supply. Similarly, low prices lead to an investment drought.

The USA has become the world's largest oil producer. Though it does not export crude oil, it now imports much less, creating a lot of spare supply. United States domestic production has nearly doubled over the six years to 2014.

The market is far from perfect and, although the **OPEC** cartel has less influence on prices, the biggest players remain Saudi Arabia and their Gulf allies. They have decided not to sacrifice their own market share. Saudi officials have said that if they cut production and prices go up, they will lose market share and merely benefit their competitors. The Saudis expect other producers to fill the gap if they reduce production.

In 2014 OPEC failed to reach agreement on production curbs, sending the price tumbling.

Market factors

Q5: Put the following market factors into the correct column in the table below:

Go online

- Cold winter in the northern hemisphere;
- Increasing miles per gallon of modern cars;
- Libya described as a "failed state";
- Reduced economic growth in China;
- Soaring shale oil production in USA.

Supply	Demand

....

3.5   The impact of oil prices on the Scottish economy

Tax revenues from oil and gas have overwhelmingly come from the Scottish sector (85-94% in recent years). Relative to the tax base of Scotland, these would be large and volatile revenues, but in the context of the UK these revenues are less significant. Declines in production and larger capital allowances have recently reduced tax revenues.

The OBR projects falling tax revenues as it predicts relatively low prices and production. The Scottish Government is more optimistic and expects a revival of these revenues based on higher prices and increased production. Changes in oil prices, production levels and capital allowances all have an impact on the oil-related activities which concentrate around centres such as Aberdeen and Shetland.

It is worth considering whether the overall impact of lower oil prices on the economy of the UK (and perhaps to a lesser extent, Scotland) will be advantageous.

Here are a few points to consider:

- Falling petrol prices left consumers with additional income to dispose of in other ways. This expenditure may have contributed to the increase in economic growth in late 2014 / early 2015 (which was convenient for a government heading into an election).

- Economic growth is good for employment.

- The reduced inflation stemming from falling petrol prices would increase real incomes.

- Reduced inflation will also delay a rise in interest rates, assisting borrowers and investors.

- Productivity in the North Sea may increase as a result of cost-cutting economies and this may further extend the life of many fields.

Many jobs have been lost in the oil sector of the economy, and you should consider this through the following two activities.

North Sea job loss announcements

Q6: Online find at least two examples of job loss announcements related to the North Sea during 2015.

. . . .

Q7: Consider the multiplier effect arising from these job losses.

. . . .

3.6 Summary

Summary

You should now be able to:

- describe recent economic trends in the oil industry;
- explain oil price fluctuations;
- evaluate the impact of oil price changes on the Scottish economy;
- update all data with the latest information from respected sources.

3.7 End of topic test

End of Topic 3 test

Go online

Q8: During most of 2014 oil prices were often:

a) above $120.
b) between $100 and $120.
c) between $60 and $100.
d) below $60.

....

Q9: Using the expected boundary line in the North Sea between Scotland and the rest of the UK, the proportion of oil production that takes place in the Scottish section of the North Sea in recent years is:

a) between 50% and 60%.
b) between 60% and 75%.
c) between 75% and 90%.
d) over 90%.

....

Q10: The demand for oil depends on:

a) the weather in oil-producing regions.
b) political stability in oil-producing nations.
c) economic growth around the world.
d) changes in capital allowances that reduce taxes on oil.

....

Q11: The supply of oil depends on:

a) new technology for developing shale oil.
b) the reduced fuel consumption of modern vehicles.
c) energy conservation measures.
d) economic growth in China.

....

Q12: Lower oil prices could benefit the UK economy by:

i   reducing inflationary pressure.

ii   increasing consumption in other areas of the economy.

iii improving productivity in the North Sea.

a) i) and ii) only
b) i) and iii) only
c) ii) and iii) only
d) all of the above

....

Topic 4

Global economic issues: globalisation (Unit 2)

Contents

Prerequisite knowledge

This topic assumes no previous knowledge and is intended to be accessible for those studying Economics for the first time. However, if you have already completed Higher Economics you will be familiar with some of the concepts outlined.

Learning objectives

By the end of this topic you should be able to:

- *explain the concept of globalisation;*

- *analyse the benefits of globalisation and the problems it may bring;*

- *analyse the reasons (including globalisation) for the rapid economic growth of China;*

- *research effectively a wide range of economic data.*

4.1 Introduction

The twin catalysts for the recent surge in **globalisation** appear to have been the revolution in information and communication technologies combined with the rampant and universal capitalism that has followed the acceptance of markets by the formerly centrally planned socialist economies such as Russia and China.

Global trade routes

The world's economies have developed ever-closer links in the process known as globalisation. China and India have made big steps forward and by their sheer size are prominent in the process, but among smaller countries such as Taiwan and Vietnam, globalisation continues apace. Taiwan is an excellent example of an open market economy that began to thrive in the 1960s, and seems to have embraced the concept of globalisation even before the term had been coined. The deregulation of markets, the development of free trade in goods and capital markets, and improvements in transport and communications have generated a vast increase in prosperity in some previously poor countries.

Globalisation

Go online

Watch a short video on YouTube entitled 'Did you know 3.0?' (https://youtu.be/YmwwrG V_aiE) giving a flavour of globalisation (video last updated 2012).

. . . .

4.2 Definitions of globalisation

Globalisation has many definitions. Collins dictionary suggests globalisation is the "process enabling financial and investment markets to operate internationally, largely as a result of **deregulation** and improved communications".

The United Nations body, ESCWA (Economic and Social Commission for Western Asia), states globalisation "when used in an economic context refers to the reduction and removal of barriers between national borders in order to facilitate the flow of goods, capital, services and labour. . . although considerable barriers remain to the flow of labour."

Globalisation has been compared to living in a world without frontiers. Increases in international trade, communications and investment have been the driving forces behind further economic integration, and the increasingly free movement of goods, capital and then people and culture in a global marketplace.

Critics denounce globalisation as leading to a world economy dominated by multinational companies that cannot be regulated by national governments.

Globalisation definition

Read the entry for globalisation on Wikipedia (http://bit.ly/1Uy5VuX).

Q1: What were the four basic aspects of globalisation identified by the IMF?

4.3 The effects of globalisation

Here are a number of economic examples of extending globalisation:

- **Multinational** companies have always been in the vanguard of globalisation, for example Ford in the USA and BP in the UK. Now the process has accelerated, expanded, and is inclusive of newly industrialised countries so that examples include Tata of India owning the UK's Jaguar brand.

- Global brand recognition was once the territory of a few iconic brands such as Ford or Coca Cola which, for many years, would have been largely unrecognised in China, the world's most populated nation. Now the list of global brands extends, and the opening of formerly planned economies to markets and private enterprise has made them truly global.

- In the car industry, components are sourced from around the globe. Throughout business, globalisation has seen a willingness to source parts and products from around the world, and the cost savings are passed on to the consumer as competitive prices. Firms choose low cost locations around the globe, or outsource services such as call centre work, to India, for example.

- Another feature is the emergence of more free trade areas in the style of the EU and the extension into common standards and the free movement of labour. The clichéd example in the UK is the Polish plumber.

Worldwide financial markets have developed and regulators have still to internationalise, catch up and impose authority.

The growth of English as the international language of business continues and the vast majority of internet traffic occurs in English. China will shortly be the nation with the greatest number of English speakers.

Tata group

Q2: Find out which countries the Tata group operate in and identify some of the products they produce.

....

4.4 Analysis of the advantages of globalisation

Ten of the claimed advantages of globalisation are listed below:

1. *Improvements in standards of living*

   There is plenty of evidence to show that countries that have embraced capitalism and free markets and have enjoyed large-scale foreign direct investment have prospered. Examples from recent history include Taiwan, Brazil and Singapore. One claim is that three billion people have been lifted from poverty in the last 50 years alongside increasing globalisation.

2. *Improvements in life expectancy*

   With economic growth comes the tax base that enables government to make wholesale improvements to sanitation, drinking water supplies and health care leading to greater **life expectancy**. Government may have used foreign aid to make initial progress, and this can be the start of the virtuous cycle of economic growth and investment in public welfare. One figure quoted is that 85% of the world's population now live to at least 60 years old. This represents a rapid improvement in the outlook for many people who previously lived in abject poverty.

3. *Improvements in literacy rates*

   Spending on basic education and improving **literacy rates** is vital if a poor country is to achieve economic take-off. When government has no funds and little to tax this is a difficult process to initiate. Foreign aid will play a major part, but if a country encourages entrepreneurship and is open to foreign investment then new funds do become available to families and to government that can be invested in the education of the next generation. It can be argued that globalisation speeds up this process.

4. *Dramatic reductions in costs of production*

   Globalisation reaps the benefits of the trade theory of comparative advantage writ large. Goods and services can be produced in the most efficient, lowest cost locations, where the four factors of production plus transport costs to market are minimised. Modern communications allow UK call centres to operate in India and for multinational firms to manufacture in Vietnam. The result is that costs and prices are contained and reduced, increasing standards of living globally.

5. **The spread of new technology**

Modern technology reaches less developed countries rapidly.   The term "intermediate technology" was in use to describe the need to supply poorer countries with technology that was basic and could be operated and repaired by local people.   Globalisation, it could be argued, enables countries to pass quickly through this halfway house stage in economic development.   Modern communications and improvements in literacy and education allow up-to-date technology to reach open economies.   Multinational firms bring with them multinational advanced technologies.

6. **Improved environmental performance**

When people are poor and starving, there is little funding to deal with environmental issues. As economic growth increases, so does the possibility of diverting some of this increased income into protecting the environment. Modern technologies are often less polluting technologies.   Increased environmental awareness is a feature of globalisation.

7. **Improvements in working conditions**

Companies moving to developing countries bring jobs, higher wages and usually better working conditions compared with domestic companies. Wages are lower in developing countries than those in advanced economies, but experience in countries like Taiwan shows that as countries develop economically wages improve and the "sweat shops" and labour intensive industries change to more capital intensive and knowledge-based industries. Multinationals generally bring working conditions and workplace standards that are higher than those provided by local firms and they pay more.

8. **Greater knowledge of and respect for other cultures**

Higher levels of migration increases the awareness and, generally, the tolerance of other cultures.

9. **Extension of democracy**

The gradual improvement in human rights and the development of democratic systems of government have generally progressed alongside globalisation.

10. **Increased international cooperation**

The level of interdependence in the world economy has strengthened institutions such as the World Trade Organisation and the World Bank. Governments have cooperated to establish international rules for the conduct of the global economy.

Benefits of globalisation - video

Q3:   Watch the documentary 'Globalisation is Good - Johan Norberg on Globalisation' (https://youtu.be/12YDLZq8rT4) available on YouTube, courtesy of Channel 4. As you watch, summarise the main themes.

Go online

You can compare your summary with the themes noted in the answer.

. . . .

Benefits of globalisation

Go online

Q4: Select the appropriate missing words and phrases from the following list to complete the list of the benefits of globalisation below:

- conditions;
- costs of production;
- cultures;
- democracy;
- environmental;
- international;
- life;
- literacy;
- living;
- technology.

Benefits of globalisation:

1. Improvements in standards of ....
2. Improvements in .... expectancy
3. Improvements in .... rates
4. Dramatic reductions in ....
5. The spread of new ....
6. Improved .... performance
7. Improvements in working ....
8. Greater knowledge of and respect for other ....
9. Extension of ....
10. Increased .... cooperation

....

4.4.1 Case studies - advantages of globalisation

Life expectancy

Q5: Using the CIA World Factbook (http://1.usa.gov/1FY6ErF), find the life expectancy in the following sample countries:

a) UK, Japan and Canada - advanced economies;
b) Singapore, Taiwan and Brazil - early gainers from globalisation;
c) Vietnam - recent gainers from globalisation;
d) Kenya - where globalisation has been restrained by government policy.

....

Literacy rates

Q6: Using the CIA World Factbook (http://1.usa.gov/1FY6ErF) , find the literacy rates in the following sample countries:

Go online

a) Singapore, Taiwan and Brazil;

b) Vietnam;

c) Kenya.

....

Effect of globalisation on the Taiwan, Brazil and Singapore economies

Q7: Research the economies of Taiwan, Brazil and Singapore online to backup the assertion that globalisation has improved these countries' standards of living.

....

4.5 Analysis of the disadvantages of globalisation

Ten of the claimed disadvantages of globalisation are listed below:

1. ***Problems associated with the restructuring of economies***

   In the short term, countries will lose uncompetitive industries as they are opened up to international competition. This will cause painful economic readjustments and higher unemployment in the short term.

2. ***Widening gap between richest and poorest countries***

   In 1960, the top richest fifth of countries in the world were 30 times richer than the poorest fifth. This gap had risen to 85 times richer by 1995. Globalisation as a process has thrown up winners among those countries that can adapt, but those nations that lack the basic infrastructure to attract foreign investment have failed to progress. Advanced economies have certainly done well out of globalisation, but further down the pecking order the outcomes are more mixed.

3. ***Destruction of traditional agricultural communities***

   A traditional way of rural life can vanish forever and local customs and culture may fade. Urbanisation does come with rising living standards and people are tempted away by the promise of prosperity. This is possibly bad news for tourists and social anthropologists, but generally considered progress by those that are no longer dependent on a good harvest in order to eat.

4. ***Movement of skilled workers to the richest countries***

   As the migration of labour is freed up and gathers pace, so some countries lose skilled workers to advanced economies that pay better. However, many return home with capital and ideas. Many send money home to family.

5. *Easier spread of disease*

One example of this arises from the tobacco industry. Markets in advanced economies began to shrink in the face of adverse publicity regarding the health problems associated with smoking. Multinational companies stand accused of profiting by expanding into countries where government regulation was minimal and anti-smoking publicity barely existed. A rise in deaths due to lung cancer can be expected in these countries whereas the advanced economies will continue to see falls in such deaths.

6. *Exploitation of workers*

There is little doubt that workers employed by multinationals in developing countries enjoy lower wages, conditions and protection than those employed in advanced economies. Health and safety standards are weaker and long hours are worked. The pay received for sewing a garment may be less than 1% of the retail price it attains in the advanced economy.

7. *Use of child labour*

Even when multinationals make clear that they do not want child labour employed they are unable to monitor the activities of their suppliers closely at all times. Investigative television reporting revealed that the sequins on the cheap clothing of one major UK discount chain could have been sewn on by children.

8. *Unskilled workers in advanced economies face competition*

For UK workers, having knowledge and skills has never been more important. Unskilled and semi-skilled jobs have been exported to developing countries along with swathes of manufacturing. Wages in unskilled jobs come under pressure from foreign workers who can undercut them.

9. *Recessions may become global*

When the world economy is interlinked, the danger of a recession affecting the whole globe at the same time is greater. When Europe and the USA start buying less, then China will produce less and so recession is quickly exported. This would be the theory, but you may care to check whether China's economy shrunk in the aftermath of the 2007-08 financial crisis.

10. *Environmental damage*

Weak and corrupt government can leave the door open for environmental damage to forests and agricultural land. For example, mining can be very polluting and modern fishing methods may ruin stocks.

Globalisation advantages and disadvantages

Q8: Put the following advantages and disadvantages of globalisation into the correct column in the table below:

Go online

- Destruction of traditional agricultural communities;
- Dramatic reductions in costs of production;
- Easier spread of disease;
- Environmental damage;
- Exploitation of workers;
- Extension of democracy;
- Greater knowledge of and respect for other cultures;
- Improved environmental performance;
- Improvements in life expectancy;
- Improvements in literacy rates;
- Improvements in standards of living;
- Improvements in working conditions;
- Increased international cooperation;
- Movement of skilled workers to richest countries;
- Problems associated with the restructuring of economies;
- Recessions may become global;
- The spread of new technology;
- Unskilled workers in advanced economies face competition;
- Use of child labour;
- Widening gap between richest and poorest countries.

Advantages	Disadvantages

. . . .

4.6   Globalisation: the Chinese experience

It is over a quarter of a century since communist China introduced free market reforms. Chinese Prime Minister, Mr Wen Jiabao, praised the Scottish eighteenth century economist Adam Smith in speeches and meetings with western journalists. He informed the Financial Times that he was carrying Smith's 'The Theory of Moral Sentiments' in his suitcase.

Mr Wen Jiabao was particularly keen on the section that explains that economic development must be shared by all otherwise it is "morally unsound" as well as threatening social stability.

Adam Smith's work

Go online

As an advanced higher student, you may be interested in accessing Adam Smith's work 'The Theory of Moral Sentiments'. The full text will be available on the internet, or you could read one of the summaries.

This is not relevant to your current topic of globalisation and is entirely optional.

. . . .

China's approach to globalisation has been cautious. Initially China protected its huge home market which hardly makes it a typical example of globalisation at work. Since joining the WTO (World Trade Organisation), China has opened itself to more trade. However international trade remains a small proportion of the overall Chinese economy.

China's strategy has been to offer a low-wage manufacturing base to attract foreign investment. The coastal area of China has done far better than the vast inland provinces. China's rapid economic growth has led to overcapacity in many industries. The impact has been felt in other countries with corporate profits falling and the formation of defensive mergers to eliminate competition.

In 2014 economic growth was 7%. Halfway through 2015 the annualised growth in factory output was 6%. Investment in fixed assets (often property) has grown at 11%.

These figures are a slowdown, but nowhere near a recession.

China has responded to market conditions by cutting interest rates and taking steps to boost domestic demand and increase imports. They claim to be moving towards a more market-based economic system by offering shares in giant state-owned conglomerates to private investors.

China's economy

Go online

Q9:   What would attract multinational companies to China?

. . . .

Q10: Which statistic above suggests that living standards in China are growing rapidly?

. . . .

India's economy

Go online

Q11: Investigate how globalisation has impacted on India.

. . . .

4.7 Summary

Summary

You should now be able to:

- explain the concept of globalisation;

- analyse the benefits of globalisation and the problems it may bring;

- analyse the reasons (including globalisation) for the rapid economic growth of China;

- research effectively a wide range of economic data.

4.8   End of topic test

End of Topic 4 test

Go online

Q12: Claimed benefits of globalisation do *not* include:

a) longer life expectancy.
b) increased literacy rates.
c) a reduction in global warming.
d) the spread of modern technology.

. . . .

Q13: As a result of globalisation, you would expect increases in:

a) tariffs.
b) labour mobility.
c) costs of production.
d) all of the above.

. . . .

Q14: Globalisation describes a process that has come about through:

a) the lowering of transport costs due to containerisation.
b) the growth of global brands marketed internationally.
c) improvements in communication technology.
d) all of the above.

. . . .

Q15: Analyse the impact of globalisation on the UK economy. *(20 marks)*

. . . .

Topic 5

Global economic issues: the European Union (Unit 2)

Contents

Prerequisite knowledge

This topic assumes no previous knowledge and is intended to be accessible for those studying Economics for the first time. However, if you have already completed Higher Economics you will be familiar with some of the concepts outlined.

Learning objectives

By the end of this topic you should be able to:

- *analyse the problems facing the eurozone;*

- *understand the difficulties faced by any nation leaving the eurozone;*

- *analyse the benefits and disadvantages of joining the eurozone;*

- *discuss the benefits and disadvantages of further EU enlargement with particular reference to Turkey;*

- *explain the aims of reforms to the Common Agricultural Policy;*

- *research effectively and analyse a wide range of economic data.*

5.1   Introduction

This topic, as with other topics in this unit, has been selected in the expectation that it will continue to be a topical issue in Economics for some years ahead. It provides useful background on the EU which is expected to continue to throw up opportunities for dissertation topics in the future. For example, at the time of writing the possible exit of Greece from the **euro** would be a topical issue.

Be aware of the need to use up-to-date source material to supplement the information here. You will also need to monitor with your teacher whether this topic does, as hoped, remain relevant for some years.

The original six EU countries have gradually grown to 28 members. as shown in the table below.

Year	Nations Joining	Total Membership
1957	Belgium, France, Italy, Luxembourg, Netherlands, West Germany	6
1973	Denmark, Eire, United Kingdom	9
1981	Greece	10
1986	Portugal, Spain	12
1995	Austria, Finland, Sweden	15
2004	Cyprus, Czech Republic, Estonia, Hungary, Latvia, Lithuania, Malta, Poland, Slovakia, Slovenia	25
2007	Bulgaria, Rumania	27
2013	Croatia	28

EU enlargement

Expansion of the EU

Q1: Which 11 EU countries adopted the euro in 1999? Find this information using a reliable source on the internet.

. . . .

Q2: Which eight countries had joined these 11 countries in the eurozone by early 2015?

. . . .

5.2   Pressures on the eurozone

Since their economies converged and many of the nations of Europe adopted the single currency, economic divergence in the **eurozone** has increased again. This has brought pressures on the euro single currency that have been accentuated by recession in 2009. This issue for the eurozone is likely to remain topical for some years. The pressures facing the eurozone are:

1. The single currency requires a single interest rate throughout the eurozone. For Spain, Greece and Ireland this interest rate was too low to quell inflationary, overheating economies. Germany, on the other hand, could have a lower interest rate. German unit labour costs rose only 5% over the euro's first decade, but Greek unit labour costs went up by 35%. In Spain and Italy, unit labour costs rose by 25%. What this clearly indicates is economies that are diverging. Under the old multi-currency system, the German mark would revalue and the Greek drachma would devalue; but this is no longer possible. Greek exports stay less competitive.

2. The fiscal position of the various governments has also been diverging. The weaker countries may need the support of the stronger countries. Greece has to pay far more than Germany to borrow money. Lending to the Greek government is considered riskier, so the interest rate is higher to reflect this. (It is worth noting that before the euro it was not unusual for the interest rate differential to be high - as much as 6% higher for the 1990s Italian economy.)

European Central Bank (ECB)

Research the euro by visiting the European Central Bank (ECB) website (http://bit.ly/1b gDXvk) and find the link for 'The Euro'.

5.2.1 The immediate outlook for the euro

Will countries quit the euro? Or will they find policies that enable them to re-establish **convergence**? Or will they just suffer economically for several years without effective policies to lift their economies, but determined to stay inside the euro. These are the three possible outcomes.

At the time of writing Greece appears to have chosen the third option, but it is possible that they may yet quit the euro. The IMF are trying to press them into economic policies that might help them re-establish convergence.

Leaving the euro seems unlikely. Politically, the negative fallout of withdrawing from the euro would seem likely to hit governments hard at the polls. It would seem like an admission of failure, even of second-class status, and would be hard to sell to voters, especially as it would seem to come as a last resort. Economics often takes a back seat to politics.

5.2.2 Leaving the euro or re-establishing convergence

Precedents in leaving a single currency

There are precedents in leaving a single currency. The Czech Republic split from Slovakia and their single currency separated. There have been similar experiences in the break-up of the old Yugoslavia. There are perhaps even parallels with the Irish Republic which maintained parity for the punt with sterling for many years (until 1979).

So, the break-up of common currencies is not new. It can happen and shouldn't be dismissed. Particularly, as a deep recession can lead to seismic political changes, and it is feasible that an election in one country could be won by an outsider or newcomer proposing to leave the euro.

Costs of leaving the euro

However, leaving the euro presents some practical problems in terms of cost:

- It is likely that only a nation in considerable economic difficulties would want to leave the euro. This could cause its new currency to decline in value from the moment of issue. The exchange rate at creation would have to be defendable, or the speculators would move in to make a killing. Supporting the new currency (devalued at birth) would be expensive. A life jacket from the IMF or the World Bank would be required, and they would only give help if the country reformed its economy (e.g. labour markets, privatisation) and reduced its fiscal deficit. If the country could do that, it wouldn't have to leave the euro in the first place;

- Borrowing money against this unstable economic backdrop would be expensive. The government would have to pay high interest rates;

- Vending machines may require modification, although it is possible to have new currency of the same size and weight as the euro. Computers would need reprogramming - the keyboards will need to produce a new currency symbol;

- A run on the banks of those leaving the euro is a big risk. The currency value would be redenominated on the changeover day, and the international value of the new denomination may plummet. Investors would seek a safe haven for their money in an established and stable currency. The already weak government fiscal position that would be part of the reason for leaving the euro would not help the government to bail out the banks.

Leaving the euro smoothly would take a lot of planning and some good fortune.

Re-establishing convergence

A far more likely outcome is that nations will remain in the euro but put their economies through a painful adjustment process. For an example of this, look at the 2009 Irish budget and the wholesale fiscal adjustments made in it. The danger here is that aggregate demand will fall further, worsening the recession. Then, the fiscal position may further deteriorate with unemployment and social benefits rising against a background of falling tax receipts.

If re-establishing convergence with the stronger euro economies is difficult, the third outcome is long-term stagnation for the weaker members. A period of low economic growth will follow unless the stronger economies boost their consumption with a large fiscal stimulus.

Other more extreme possibilities include some governments defaulting on debt, and choosing either to stay with or leave the euro in the aftermath.

Single currency options

Q3: Research information on the options available for nations wishing to leave the eurozone. A starting point may be to search online for "should Greece leave the Euro?"

Go online

....

Q4: Search the web to find an article that explains how Czechoslovakia divided its currency into two separate currencies when it split into the Czech Republic and Slovakia.

....

5.3 The advantages and disadvantages of euro membership

Benefits of euro membership include:

1. *Transaction costs* - There will be no costs involved in changing currencies. Firms and tourists will benefit from this. Attempts to quantify this benefit suggest a once and for all gain of about 1% of GDP.

2. **Price transparency** - It will be easier to compare prices throughout the eurozone because they would all be in euros. Firms and consumers would find cheaper raw materials and goods. With a single currency consumers would notice these price differentials and firms would come under pressure to reduce them.

3. *Reducing exchange rate uncertainty* - Firms trading with, but not in, the eurozone have enough uncertainty to handle with normal business risk and economic cycles. At present, over and above these risks, there is the chance of the euro exchange rate moving against them and ruining profits all on its own. Joining the euro single currency reduces the risk from volatile exchange rates and should lead to greater trade and economic growth.

4. *Reducing the risk of inflation* - The theory was that German discipline (paranoia?) about inflation would ensure that the European Central Bank would set a strong line with interest rates to confine inflation.

5. *Inward investment* - If the plan is to export to the eurozone, then this should be more attractive without transaction costs and with no exchange rate volatility.

6. *Impact on the financial sector* - Trading in eurozone shares would be made easier. Insurance and banking would have a similar opportunity to develop in foreign markets.

The disadvantages include:

1. *Loss of independent control of monetary policy* - The European Central Bank and the interest rate it sets could be out of line with a particular nation's economic needs.

2. *Impact on the housing market* - In the case of UK entry, the significance of interest rate changes for the UK economy is greater because of the UK's focus on house purchase rather than rental. This adds weight to the argument for the UK to retain control of interest rates by not joining the eurozone.

3. **Changeover costs** - The initial costs of changing currency are large - vending and slot machine changes are one example.

4. **Loss of devaluation option** - Devaluation is removed from a nation's economic policy options, so they would no longer be able to stimulate their economy by devaluing the currency and increasing exports. If they can't remain convergent with stronger economies (if for example wage costs rise) it will need to deflationary fiscal policies to compensate. The euro is essentially a fixed exchange rate arrangement, and in time may be subject to the same pressures from diverging economies that fixed rates have always been subject to. With the added pressure of recession, Spain, Portugal and Greece would all have benefitted from a lower exchange rate relative to other countries, but no such option existed for them.

5. **Loss of independent fiscal policy** - The EU's growth and stability pact would limit government borrowing to 3% of GDP. Increased regional aid within Europe will be needed to offset economic inequalities that can no longer be addressed through national currency realignments. Richer nations will be net contributors to this funding. If some eurozone members increase their borrowings and national debt, this will lead to the single interest rate rising throughout the zone.

6. **Unexpected events** - Over time, a number of unexpected events can be expected. These events will be of different significance for each eurozone economy. They will make these economies diverge. For example, the "credit crunch" had a disproportionate effect on countries such as the UK and Ireland where the banking and financial sectors are a larger part of the total economy. If oil prices soared then net importers of oil such as France and Germany would be far more affected than the UK with its North Sea production. Policy responses for these "shocks" could usefully involve interest rates, but within the one size fits all eurozone interest rates, this option is not available.

Advantages and disadvantages of joining the eurozone

Go online

Q5: Decide whether the following statements are advantages or disadvantages of joining the eurozone:

- Devaluation of national currency no longer possible;
- Easier for consumers to compare prices in different countries;
- Exchange rate certainty for firms within eurozone;
- Fiscal policy subject to strict rules that limit ability to borrow in recession;
- Multinational investment more likely;
- No commission on changing currency;
- One interest rate set for all of eurozone;
- Unexpected events may lead to eurozone economies diverging.

Advantages	Disadvantages

. . . .

5.4   EU enlargement

EU **enlargement** is the process of widening the EU through the admission of new members. The EU project started in 1957 with six member states and now it has enlarged six times and by 2015 it had 28 member nations.

Around the edges of the current map, the Balkan states formed on the break-up Yugoslavia will shortly be looking for entry (e.g. Serbia). Turkey has long been interested, but is perhaps not as close to membership now as a few years ago. North African countries just across the Mediterranean have historic links to many European countries and are also possible members.

Switzerland retains an independent outlook and has historically sought to remain neutral, with secretive Swiss banks perhaps preferring not to have European Union laws applied to them. Norway voted against entry when its Scandinavian neighbours joined. It has a small population similar to Scotland and its immense oil reserves make it very prosperous outside the EU. Also, its important fishing industry does not have to abide by EU policies.

5.4.1   Recent EU enlargement

When Romania and Bulgaria joined the EU in 2007, the European Commission said that they brought the following advantages:

- rapidly growing economies - about 6% a year;

- a highly motivated workforce;

- a potential link between the EU and Balkan and Black Sea areas.

Romania and Bulgaria have 6% of the EU population and less than 1% of the EU GDP. They are the poorest members of the EU with GDP per head running at a third of the EU average. Entry was allowed despite concerns over corruption and organised crime, the assumption being that allowing them in would assist reform in these areas.

Future candidates for membership include:

- Albania;

- Bosnia and Herzegovina;

- Kosovo;

- Macedonia;

- Montenegro;

- Serbia;

- Turkey.

EU treaties allow any European country to apply if it meets conditions, such as:

- a market economy;

- the rule of law;

- respect for human rights;

- democracy.

5.4.2 The case for and against EU enlargement

Following entry, new members receive more from the EU than they pay into the budget. Bulgaria and Romania received about 1.5bn euros in pre-entry assistance.

However, many of the older EU members (e.g. Spain, Greece, Portugal and Ireland) also end up with net gains from membership. In fact, Spain received more in 2005 than the 10 new member states combined.

There are greater gains for all from membership of the **single market** that are far more significant than making a net gain from the EU budget and these do not enter the calculations.

Benefits of EU enlargement

The process of enlargement has several benefits for the UK:

- provides consumers with a greater choice of products, as new members begin to export to the UK;

- increases competition which drives down prices, leads to innovative behaviour by firms and can improve the quality of products;

- allows labour shortages to be met with foreign workers. This addition to supply in the labour market will help to keep down wage inflation, which is good news for companies and a benefit for the overall economy;

- provides new markets (no trade barriers) for our exports and exporters should gain more from economies of scale as they supply a free trade single market of nearly 500 million consumers;

- provides opportunities for UK-based firms to improve profitability by moving to the lower wage economies of the new members.

Problems with EU enlargement

The process of enlargement also creates problems for the UK:

- UK workers will face more competition in the labour market and their wages are less likely to rise. (However, unemployment may not rise, because much of the money earned by foreign workers will be spent in the UK and thus they create jobs as well as take jobs.)

- subsidies for the economic development of the new members may be expensive for richer countries such as the UK. The UK will be a net contributor to the EU budget through the CAP and regional aid.

- firms may move manufacturing to the new member countries to take advantage of lower costs (e.g. wages) and this will lead to some job losses in the UK.

EU enlargement

Put the following words into place in the paragraph below:

Go online

- choice;

- competition;

- foreign workers;

- job losses;

- manufacturing;

- prices;

- profitability;

- quality;

- subsidies;

- wages.

Q6: For the UK the process of enlargement has several benefits. Consumers will have a greater .... of products. This increases .... which drives down ....
, leads to innovative behaviour by firms, and can improve the .... of products. Enlargement allows labour shortages to be met with .... and keeps down wage inflation. It provides opportunities for UK based firms to improve .... by moving to the lower wage economies of the new members.

Enlargement can create problems. UK workers will face more competition in the labour market and their .... are less likely to rise. Regional aid and CAP .... for the economic development of the new members may be expensive. Firms may move .... and some service jobs to the new member countries to take advantage of lower wages and this will lead to some .... in the UK.

....

5.4.3 Turkey

Of all the potential entrants, Turkey provides the most interesting case. The remaining non-EU European nations have fairly small populations and while the political operation and decision-making of an increasingly numerous EU state count may be difficult, at least from an economic viewpoint the absorption of these countries should follow established models.

The Helsinki European Council of December 1999 granted Turkey candidate status. Accession negotiations started in October 2005 after reforms that included:

- the abolition of the death penalty;

- protections against torture;

- greater freedom of expression and increased respect for minorities.

Turkey is special, and worthy of study as a case on its own, as:

1. it links Europe to Asia;

2. its democracy has looked unstable at times and EU membership would entrench democracy in Turkey. This would improve stability, security and prosperity in that region;

3. it is a populous nation that, with a market economy and globalisation, has the potential to be a significant economic power;

4. it provides links to energy sources to the East;

5. it greatly expands the single market and embraces globalisation for existing EU members. Politically, the EU acting as one would be an even more powerful block.

There are stumbling blocks. For example, further progress is required on:

- women's rights;

- anti-corruption measures;

- judicial reform;

- agricultural reform;

- freedom of expression and the rights of minority religious groups.

Turkey also does not recognise Cyprus and this means it cannot open its ports and airports to all EU member states.

Turkey - EU membership

Q7: Summarise the benefits that the membership of Turkey may bring to the EU. *(6 marks)*

Go online

. . . .

Q8: Summarise the outstanding issues that have to be dealt with before the EU will give final consideration to Turkey's application. *(6 marks)*

. . . .

Turkey's current economic performance

Q9: Investigate the current economic performance of Turkey by going to the CIA World Factbook (http://1.usa.gov/1FY6ErF) .

. . . .

Make notes on the variations between the economic and social data on Turkey compared to a major EU country such as Germany.

. . . .

5.5   Reform of the Common Agricultural Policy (CAP)

The **Common Agricultural Policy (CAP)** is the biggest item of EU expenditure, costing the UK several billion a year in subsidy and increasing food costs. It uses up a large proportion of the EU budget. France enjoys the largest share of CAP funds. Ireland and Greece also receive a large share, relative to their economic size.

The CAP hits the world's poorest countries by subsidising their high-cost competitors in the EU. It does not adequately protect the natural environment. Much of the money goes to agribusiness and not to the poorest farmers.

Subsidised products include olives, fruit, vegetables, sugar and wine. Costs running into billions of euros are paid to olive farmers and to sugar producers. In one year the biggest gainer from the CAP in the UK was the sugar company Tate and Lyle with a donation from the EU of €186 million. The Queen has received approximately €500,000 per year!

The subsidies distort world markets and harm farmers in developing countries by guaranteeing good prices for farmers in the EU. For further protection, tariffs are added to the price of imports.

One notorious example of an EU subsidy was in the sugar market. The world price for sugar was £144 per tonne, but the EU had a minimum guaranteed price of £432 - almost three times as much.

Recent changes build on a major CAP reform process started in 2003. This broke the link between farm production and subsidies. The current objective is to move funding into rural development and conservation measures and to leave agriculture more responsive to market forces.

Reform of the EU intends to encourage farmers to move away from dependency on subsidies and promote sustainable and diverse rural communities.

Common Agricultural Policy (CAP)

Research the latest information on reform of the CAP. The official EU website (http://eur opa.eu/index_en.htm) is a useful starting point.

. . . .

5.6   Summary

Summary

You should now be able to:

- analyse the problems facing the eurozone;

- understand the difficulties faced by any nation leaving the eurozone;

- analyse the benefits and disadvantages of joining the eurozone;

- discuss the benefits and disadvantages of further EU enlargement with particular reference to Turkey;

- explain the aims of reforms to the Common Agricultural Policy;

- research effectively and analyse a wide range of economic data.

5.7　End of topic test

End of topic 5 test

Q10: Which country joined the EU in 2013?

Go online

a) Switzerland
b) Russia
c) Croatia
d) Norway

....

Q11: How many nations are currently (2015) in the EU?

a) 15
b) 21
c) 25
d) 28

....

Q12: Which of the following nations was a founding member of the EU?

a) Italy
b) United Kingdom
c) Spain
d) Denmark

....

Q13: Which two countries joined the EU in 2007?

a) Slovenia and Slovakia
b) Latvia and Lithuania
c) Romania and Bulgaria
d) Croatia and Serbia

....

Q14: The initials CAP stand for:

a) Current Agricultural Policy
b) Common Agricultural Policy
c) Current Accession Procedure
d) Common Accession Procedure

....

Q15: EU enlargement refers to the process of:

a) creating of a greater number of common standards throughout the EU.
b) economic growth creating greater European gross domestic product.
c) establishing wider powers for the European Parliament.
d) the widening of the EU by allowing in new member nations.

....

Q16: Which of the following (as of 2015) is a eurozone member state?

a) United Kingdom
b) Portugal
c) Sweden
d) Denmark

....

Q17: Two problems with allowing Turkey to join the EU is that: *(choose the two options that apply)*

a) part of Turkey is in Asia.

b) the death penalty still exists in Turkey.

c) further progress is required on women's rights.

d) it must become a democracy first.

....

Q18: One advantage for the UK in joining the eurozone is the ability to:

a) devalue the currency so as to compete better in the eurozone.
b) set interest rates to suit the needs of our economy.
c) easily compare UK prices with those of other eurozone nations.
d) budget for a large fiscal deficit if the economy requires it.

....

Topic 6

Economic growth in developing and emerging economies (Unit 2)

Contents

Learning objectives

By the end of this topic you should be able to:

- *explain reasons for varying rates of economic growth in developing economies;*

- *explain reasons for varying rates of economic growth in emerging economies;*

- *research effectively and analyse a wide range of economic data.*

6.1   Emerging economies

There is no established convention on the definition of the terms **developing economy** and **emerging economy**. Also, many similar terms co-exist, e.g. least developed economies, tiger economies, BRIC economies.

One recent addition to the terms used to describe emerging economies is 'EAGLES' which is an acronym for Emerging and Growth Leading Economies. This current EAGLE membership, in the table below, provides a useful list for our term emerging economies.

Bangladesh	Nigeria
Brazil	Pakistan
China	Philippines
India	Russia
Indonesia	Saudi Arabia
Iraq	Thailand
Mexico	Turkey

EAGLE membership (as of 2014)

For the purposes of this course there are three divisions broadly judged by their GDP per capita, viz:

- advanced economies (e.g. USA);

- emerging economies (e.g. Brazil);

- developing economies (e.g. Malawi).

Many countries are transitioning up the divisions, and therefore it is best to select clear-cut examples as above and to avoid the grey areas of transition in between.

An emerging economy is a nation with some characteristics of an advanced economy but is not yet an advanced economy. These nations have business and economic activity in the process of rapid growth and industrialization. They are clearly more prosperous than developing economies as can be judged by statistics for GDP per capita, literacy rates and life expectancy rates.

World factbook - emerging economies

Q1:   Find the GDP per capita of Brazil and India using the World Factbook section of the CIA website (http://1.usa.gov/1KyForg).

Then find two other 'EAGLE' nations with broadly similar GDP per capita figures.

. . . .

6.2   Developing economies

According to the International Monetary Fund's World Economic Outlook Report (April 2015) there are 152 countries considered to be developing economies (http://bit.ly/1Jw EGIL).

Immediately, we have a definition problem. The IMF (International Monetary Fund), the World Bank and the United Nations are just three of the august institutions that cannot agree on a definition of the terms in this area. Hence the list of countries is of limited use.

World factbook - developing economies

Q2:   Find the GDP per capita of Malawi and Chad using the World Factbook section of the CIA website (http://1.usa.gov/1KyForg).

Then find two other nations from the list of developing economies with broadly similar GDP per capita figures.

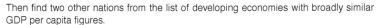

6.3   Factors that delay economic growth

When it comes to the problems facing less developed countries, one approach is to take the four factors of production in turn and recite quality and quantity issues they face.

The following may give you an initial understanding of the roots of their problems:

- **Natural resources** (Land) will not be fertile. Either the climate or the soil type will prevent it from producing plenty. If it is fertile, then it may be prone to seasonal flooding or drought. Crop yields will either be low or not reliable. Agriculture will dominate many of these economies with perhaps 80% of the workforce engaged in farming.

  Mineral deposits will be limited or difficult to access. Those mines that do exist will be owned by multinationals and the workers may be poorly paid with the profits going to shareholders in developed countries. Political instability and corruption may prevent the returns from valuable mineral deposits trickling down to the general population.

- **Human resources** (Labour) will not be skilled. The education system will be poor and literacy rates low. As a result, labour productivity will be low and foreign investment will not be attracted other than to exploit valuable mineral deposits. Workers may be weakened by malnutrition or disease.

  Life expectancy will be low. There may be a burgeoning young population of dependents but quite a small population of working age. The number of able workers of working age will be restricted by health issues. In many parts, HIV and Aids are significantly affecting many families.

- **Man-made resources** (Capital) will be of poor quality. Operating at near subsistence level there will be no surplus put aside to assist with future production. Machinery will tend to be cheap and basic when it does exist. The lack of social capital and infrastructure such as roads and harbours will make the country unattractive to foreign investors.

A lack of savings will lead to a lack of funds being recycled into investment. The banking system will be poor. Foreign investment is badly needed to kick-start economic development.

- **Entrepreneurs** (Enterprise) will exist on a small scale in local markets. Any excess farm output will find its way to a market stall. The growth of enterprise is dependent on the availability of capital to invest, and partly on the education levels of the entrepreneurs.

  The number of entrepreneurs and the size of companies will be restricted by the small incomes of consumers, and the inadequacies of the banking system.

These problems with the four factors of production lead to long term problems with economic development.

Go online

Factors that delay economic growth

Q3:   Match the following quality and quantity issues to each factor of production in the table below:

- bureaucratic "red tape";
- inadequate roads;
- low rainfall;
- poor health;
- limited skills;
- little savings;
- few business skills;
- few natural resources.

Land	Labour	Capital	Enterprise

. . . .

6.4   Economic growth and stage of economic development

A brief look at the historic statistics in the table below reveals a pattern. Both emerging and developing economies are growing more rapidly than advanced economies (percentages rounded to nearest half per cent).

Type of economy	2007	2008	2009	2010
Emerging and developing	9%	6%	2.5%	7.5%
Advanced	2.5%	0%	-3.5%	3%
Total world growth	5%	3%	-0.5%	5%

Economic growth and type of economy

Note that the growth rates of emerging and developing countries should not be considered in isolation from population growth. GDP per capita tends to rise more slowly than GDP.

Economic growth of developing and emerging economies

Q4: Obtain the most up-to-date figures available on the internet for the economic growth of developing and emerging economies.

. . . .

The important factors that influence the rate of economic growth in developing countries are:

- improvements in education, especially primary education and the accompanying increase in literacy and numeracy;

- improvements in sanitation and health care, which lead to lower infant mortality, increased life expectancy and fitter, more productive workers;

- political stability - improvements in the legal system and an absence of civil war or international conflict;

- diversification away from reliance on a single primary product.

Emerging economies have these pre-conditions for growth in place and continue to improve education and health services. Emerging economies with the highest growth rates will have:

- high levels of private investment in business - much of it from foreign multinationals;

- high levels of investment by government in major infrastructure projects such as improvements to transport links;

- an economy rapidly diversifying into manufacturing;

- moves towards free trade and internationally open markets;

- the encouragement of entrepreneurship and a preference for free market solutions over state intervention;

- relaxed labour laws (workers are poorly protected from exploitation) and very competitive hourly wage rates.

Economic growth of developing and emerging economies

Go online

Q5: What are the three most important pre-conditions for the initial economic growth of developing countries?

. . . .

Q6: Suggest three further factors that contribute to the economic growth of emerging economies.

. . . .

6.5　Research example - the effect of falling commodity prices on Zambia

Zambia was the world's third largest copper producer in the 1960s. On gaining independence from the UK in 1964, it seemed destined to be one of Africa's most prosperous countries. What happened?

Map showing location of Zambia within Africa

In 1975 the world copper price slumped. Despite the undermining effect this had on the Zambian economy, it remained the country's biggest export earner. Zambia was unable to diversify sufficiently, and although agriculture and tourism also contribute to the economy, the price of copper has remained key to the country's economic development.

From the 1990s, two favourable events have assisted the Zambian copper industry. Firstly, the industry has been privatised, thus releasing the powerful profit motive and opening the door to foreign investment. Secondly, the growth of the worldwide sales of electronics led to a derived increased demand for copper.

The fundamental problem for Zambia and nations in a similar position is the over-dependence on one primary product. Zambia's economy needs to diversify. Until it has diversified, the prosperity of Zambia is closely linked to the volatile world copper price.

The price of copper has not been the only problem facing Zambia in this period. You should be able to research the other issues that faced Zambia, many of which were typical of a less developed country.

Zambia's problems

Q7: What problems have faced Zambia since independence (1964)?

A good starting point may be the Country Profiles (http://bbc.in/1Lw8tzl) section on the BBC website.

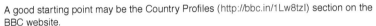

Real GDP growth in Zambia is expected to increase to over 6% in 2015. This resumes previous growth rates following 5.7% in 2013, due to reduced copper production. The country benefits from political stability, and although 60% still live in poverty, the standards of living are improving in cities and along major transport routes. A major aim of government is the diversification of the economy to reduce the dependence on copper.

Highly Indebted Poor Country (HIPC) Initiative

Q8: Use the internet to find out about the Highly Indebted Poor Country (HIPC) Initiative. How does the HIPC Initiative help these countries?

The price of copper

Q9: Find out as much as you can about the price of copper over the last few years. Comment on the variations you find.

Another developing economy

Q10: Find out about another one of the world's developing economies. What are the country's particular economics problems? To what extent does it resemble the Zambian experience?

Your starting point may be the information available through the BBC website's Country Profiles (http://bbc.in/1Lw8tzl) or through the CIA's World Factbook (http://1.usa.gov/1F Y6ErF) section.

6.6   Research example - the effect of rising energy prices on developing countries

Surprisingly, some of the world's poorest countries are oil producers. Nigeria has been a well-known oil producer for years. Less well-known are the oil reserves of Angola, Chad, Sudan and Equatorial Guinea.

Map of Africa showing five oil producing countries

The rise in energy prices should have helped these countries, but did they make good use of the extra revenues?

Equatorial Guinea is now the third largest oil exporter in sub-Saharan Africa. Despite this, most of its small population live in poverty. The same president has been in office since 1979, and the ruling elite are prosperous. According to the International Monetary Fund, Angola had no records for about $4 billion of oil revenues for the period 1997 and 2002.

Even when corruption is not the issue, these countries can lack expertise in allocating the revenues to sensible investments in infrastructure. Rising oil prices have also been blamed for increasing power struggles within these countries.

For the greater number of poor countries the problems of rising energy prices represent an intolerable additional burden, rather than the windfall they are to Angola and the oil exporters.

By 2007, oil prices had tripled in four years. In the Asian and Pacific region, this put spending on imports up by nearly $400 billion. One study of the impact on the poor in these areas states that spending on energy went up by three quarters between 2002 and 2005. The poor are faced with cutting back on other essentials in order to pay for basics such as lighting and cooking oil.

Nations with the greatest dependence on imported oil include Cambodia and Sri Lanka. Less dependent but still vulnerable are Malaysia and Thailand because of their rapidly growing demand for oil. China and India face less of a problem because of their greater use of coal, and their stronger economies can face the challenge of higher oil prices.

The effect of rising oil prices on developing countries

Q11: Explain the effect of rising oil prices on developing countries.

Go online

. . . .

6.7   Summary

Summary

You should now be able to:

- explain reasons for varying rates of economic growth in developing economies;

- explain reasons for varying rates of economic growth in emerging economies;

- research effectively and analyse a wide range of economic data.

6.8   End of topic test

End of Topic 6 test

Go online

Q12: Which of the following countries have emerging economies?   Choose **five** countries.

Brazil	Chad	China	India	Ireland
Italy	Malawi	Mali	Nigeria	Russia

....

Choose the best option to complete the following sentences regarding developing countries.

Q13: Developing countries make progress if they are able to improve the ....

a) birthrate
b) levels of literacy and numeracy
c) natural resources

....

Q14: More productive workers are possible if .... levels are improved.

a) welfare benefit
b) pension
c) sanitation

....

Q15: The economy will also need to diversify away from a dependence on a single .... product.

a) primary
b) secondary
c) tertiary

....

Q16: Describe the characteristics of emerging economies. *(6 marks)*

....

....

Topic 7

End of Unit 2 test

End of Unit 2 test

Go online

Q1: The structural deficit exists because of:

a) increased benefit spending during recession.
b) reduced income tax receipts during recession.
c) long-term investment in infrastructure by government.
d) the privatisation of public sector assets.

. . . .

Q2: The demand for oil depends on:

a) the weather in oil-producing regions.
b) political stability in oil-producing nations.
c) economic growth around the world.
d) changes in capital allowances that reduce taxes on oil.

. . . .

Q3: Lower oil prices could benefit the UK economy by:

i   reducing inflationary pressure.

ii   increasing consumption in other areas of the economy.

iii   improving productivity in the North Sea.

a) i) and ii) only
b) i) and iii) only
c) ii) and iii) only
d) all of the above

. . . .

Q4: As a result of globalisation, you would expect increases in:

a) tariffs.
b) labour mobility.
c) costs of production.
d) all of the above.

. . . .

Q5: Globalisation describes a process that has come about through:

a) the lowering of transport costs due to containerisation.
b) the growth of global brands marketed internationally.
c) improvements in communication technology.
d) all of the above.

. . . .

Q6: Greece may find it difficult to be in a common currency with Germany because:

a) the cost of transporting their exports to Germany is high.
b) they do not share a central bank.
c) inflation in Germany tends to be higher.
d) they cannot match German levels of productivity.

....

Q7: By *not* being in the Eurozone, the UK is able to:

a) impose tariffs on imports from the Eurozone.
b) avoid currency conversion costs.
c) set its own interest rates independently.
d) limit the free movement of labour from the Eurozone.

....

Q8: Economic growth in developing economies can be held back by:

I   poor health and sanitation.

II   low levels of spending on education.

III high government spending on infrastructure projects.

a) I) and II) only
b) I) and III) only
c) II) and III) only
d) I), II) and III)

....

Q9: Economic growth in emerging economies is encouraged by:

I   increasing levels of foreign investment.

II   high spending on education.

III political stability.

a) I) and II) only
b) I) and III) only
c) II) and III) only
d) I), II) and III)

....

Q10: Which of the following groups lists a developing economy, an emerging economy, and an advanced economy in that order?

a) Russia, Japan, Germany
b) Malawi, Brazil, Canada
c) India, Zambia, France
d) China, Mali, Italy

....

Q11: Explain how "austerity" policies that reduce government spending could potentially delay the achievement of a balanced budget. *(7 marks)*

. . . .

Q12: Explain the possible benefits for the UK economy of a balanced budget. *(6 marks)*

. . . .

Topic 8

How to organise your project (Unit 3)

Contents

Prerequisite knowledge

This topic assumes no previous knowledge and is intended to be accessible for those studying Economics for the first time. However, if you have already completed Higher Economics you will be familiar with some of the concepts outlined.

Learning objectives

By the end of this topic you should be able to:

- *understand the importance for your project of preparation and planning, and the need for good time management;*

- *select a suitable topic that is feasible to research and within your capabilities;*

- *research your chosen topic and analyse your research;*

- *plan and record a programme of economic research;*

- *present your project findings in an acceptable structure that relates to the marking scheme;*

- *synthesise your research into coherent conclusions and present these appropriately.*

8.1 Organisation and planning

This project produces an end document which will be an extended piece of writing that is divided into sections. You might make up your own structure, but in Advanced Higher Economics there is guidance supplied on how the marks are allocated which it would be wise to act upon.

Your project will amass the evidence from a wide range of sources that will help you to draw informed economic conclusions to a question that relates to a topical economic issue.

The unit you are undertaking when you write your project is called 'researching an economic issue'. It is one of three units in the Advanced Higher Economics course. The SQA guidance says that "the general aim of this unit is to allow learners to plan their research of a current economic issue in order to develop their economic research skills."

Your project amounts to one third of your final mark.

The good candidate will seek out their teacher for guidance, opinions and criticism. The project allows the well-organised candidate to allocate the time and effort necessary to producing a good quality piece of work. There will be sufficient time for the first draft to be checked over carefully and improved. The final document will be well-presented and standardised in style and layout. Facts will be rigorously checked for accuracy. Conclusions will be subtle and matched up with the initial aims of the project.

The rushed candidate will leave more to chance and may have no clear timetable or make minimal effort to keep to the timetable they have. As the deadline nears they will panic and their research, instead of being wide-ranging, will be aimed at finding one or two items that are ripe for plagiarising. Even if they are sufficiently talented writers, the final outcome is likely to be unsatisfying from an educational point of view and the mark will be less than they might have expected. They will have gained little from the process and they may take away the notion that they can handle future deadlines in this way.

Consider the following:

- Passing the Advanced Higher Economics course with 50% following a project that gains 30/40 requires an examination mark of 30/80 (or 37.5%).

- However, passing the course with 50% following a project that gains 15/40 requires an examination mark of 45/80 (or 56%).

- So, the high-scoring project will put you into the final exam with over a grade advantage over the weaker project. Your university entrance may depend on it - so start early and keep to your dissertation timetable.

8.2 Stages in writing up your project

The diagram below gives a simple outline of the stages you will go through in writing your project.

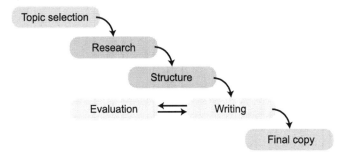

Diagram showing the stages in writing up a project

Placing the elements of the process in a sequential order does over-simplify the procedure a bit. In Economics, you may be dealing with a topic that is developing as you write. Be prepared to adjust and insert new research information as you write. Stay flexible - your final copy will be amended and improved as a result of the evaluation of your draft copy and the incorporation of information acquired late in the day.

Project plan

Q1: Devise a basic project plan using the broad stages in the diagram above and placing a timescale against them.

Go online

. . . .

8.3   Project remit

You should receive from your teacher:

- clear guidance on the upper and lower word limits;

- advice on the suitability of topics you are considering;

- some pointers on the location of suitable material for starting your research;

- the deadline date for completion (and the teacher may suggest some interim dates for the completion of different stages of the work such as the completion of a first draft).

If you want a considered opinion on your work, you will have to give your teacher sufficient time to look over your draft. This will mean you will have to meet the agreed interim deadlines. Your teacher will have many other students competing for his or her time; don't assume your teacher will give you a privileged status as an Advanced Higher candidate.

Key points for your remit:

- select an economic issue that is topical within the last 18 months;
- word count is between 3500 to 4000 words (excluding bibliography, footnotes and appendices);
- a maximum of three appendices can be included;
- confirm the due date and submit your report by this date;
- have a question as your title, rather than a statement;
- provide references for quotes and tables and graphs;
- a **bibliography** should indicate all sources of information used;
- provide a word count with the report (and a penalty is applied if it exceeds 4,400).

SQA allocate 40 marks for the project, out of a total of 120 marks for the Advanced Higher Economics course. The allocation of marks (in brackets) is broken down as follows:

1. Introduction (4);
2. Analysis and evaluation (12);
3. Conclusions (6);
4. Research (6);
5. Structure and coherence (8);
6. Presentation and referencing (4).

For fuller details access the Economics Project General Assessment Information from the SQA website (http://bit.ly/1Kbm7XD).

8.4   Selecting a topic

You should choose a topic that interests you and is within your capabilities. Always check on the ease with which you can research your topic.

The selected issue must be a current issue defined as active within the last two years.

What you don't want to produce is a mere descriptive work. This kind of report may be well-informed, represent a summary of the reading and months of studious activity, and it may show that you have a clear understanding of the topic. However it will probably lack incisiveness, individuality and personal insight. It will be an erudite study or review of the work of others, and more than a little dull.

In Advanced Higher Economics you should pick a topic that is an argument. This will be a question that lacks a definitive answer but offers several viewpoints to criticise and consider, not least your own one which you will form as your research, analysis and evaluation continues.

Your conclusions will, according to the SQA (http://bit.ly/1Kbm7XD) , "demonstrate valid judgements have been reached that are related to the issue/aim(s), and are based on the analysis and evaluation of the evidence. The reasoning behind the conclusions is fully explained." The weighting attached by you to the various conclusions will represent your informed judgement of the issue.

Selecting a topic

Q2: From the following list of topics, select those that best meet the project requirements:

- The financial crisis of 2007-08 - should the banks have been saved?
- Should the budget deficit be reduced as quickly as planned?
- The advantages and disadvantages of joining the euro.
- Should the UK join the euro?
- Why did house prices fall in 2008?
- What were the causes of the Great Depression?
- What should be the favoured currency option if Scotland gained independence?

There are some hints for this activity which you should look at *after* you have selected your suitable topics.

. . . .

8.5   Key points to consider for your project

In summary, the key points to consider for your project are as follows:

- select a current issue that interests you and phrase it as a question;
- time management is important, so agree deadlines for the completion of sections with your teacher and stick to them;
- research widely and maintain a bibliography. Watch out for developments that occur as you are writing as they may require changes to be made;
- refer closely to the way in which marks are allocated and present your project in a format that seeks to gather in these marks;
- follow the teacher's advice on layout and presentation;
- use economic theory to explain wherever possible;
- draw your conclusions from the evidence and explicitly state how the evidence leads you to your conclusions.

8.6 Summary

Summary

You should now be able to:

- understand the importance for your project of preparation and planning, and the need for good time management;

- select a suitable topic that is feasible to research and within your capabilities;

- research your chosen topic and analyse your research;

- plan and record a programme of economic research;

- present your project findings in an acceptable structure that relates to the marking scheme;

- synthesise your research into coherent conclusions and present these appropriately.

8.7 End of topic test

End of Topic 1 test

Q3: In the marks for the project, what percentage is allocated to presentation and referencing?

Go online

a) 5%
b) 10%
c) 15%

. . . .

Q4: The maximum word limit for the project is:

a) 3,000
b) 3,500
c) 4,000

. . . .

Q5: What percentage of your final course mark is allocated to your project?

a) 20%
b) 25%
c) 33%

. . . .

Q6: Your chosen topic must be both:

a) current and economically significant.
b) current and macroeconomic.
c) microeconomic and economically significant.

. . . .

Topic 9

How to research and write your project (Unit 3)

Contents

Prerequisite knowledge

This topic assumes no previous knowledge and is intended to be accessible for those studying Economics for the first time. However, if you have already completed Higher Economics you will be familiar with some of the concepts outlined.

Learning objectives

By the end of this topic you should be able to:

- *develop independent research skills;*

- *understand the difference between qualitative and quantitative research;*

- *evaluate if the range of sources used is appropriate for the needs of the research;*

- *keep an accurate record of the research process and sources used;*

- *use a referencing system and bibliography and explain the importance of them.*

9.1   Research sources

Where will you go for information on your chosen topic?

The following points can be made about your sources:

- use a range of different relevant sources;

- make sure the information is up-to-date;

- make sure your sources are sufficient to back up your findings and conclusions.

These are all **secondary** sources, but the nature of your dissertation may require you to do some field or **primary** research.

Primary research is a time-consuming process; if a questionnaire is to be used be very careful about the way in which questions are asked. Will you want to draw quantitative data from your questionnaire? This may require a tick box approach.

Qualitative or quantitative research?

Q1: Research the difference between qualitative or quantitative research.

Go online

School textbooks in Business Management are likely to cover this area in sufficient detail for your needs. In addition, there are business dictionaries available online.

....

A successful questionnaire

Q2: This activity is aimed only at those who expect to be designing a questionnaire or conducting a survey.

Go online

Research factors to remember when designing a successful questionnaire. Use the internet to find articles on this subject using the key words "questionnaire design".

....

9.1.1   Verifying sources of evidence

You should always try to judge whether your source can be trusted.

Newspapers often show a political bias, though it may not always be obvious. They may be "economical with the truth" presenting only those parts of the truth that suit their opinion. As elections approach, this bias is even greater. As a general rule, items in The Telegraph, may tend to favour political views on the right and The Guardian may favour more liberal-left views. The BBC news may be more impartial, but even it was heavily criticised in some quarters for its coverage of the Scottish referendum.

The print and television media mentioned in the previous paragraph are about as reliable as any, but you may need to look for another source to verify the "facts". It is important to use several sources and form a balanced opinion when researching.

The internet is no more reliable than the printed word. Wikipedia, for example, allows open access which means that some articles can be wrongly amended or inaccurate. Editors do check postings and remove errors, but this can take time. Therefore, always seek to confirm Wikipedia information by looking at other trusted websites.

The ONS (Office for National Statistics) is probably the best source for economic "facts" in the UK. However, like all state-run organisations, it may be influenced by government, if only indirectly through the selection of senior staff.

9.1.2 Plagiarism

A plagiarist is defined as: "someone who steals the thoughts or writings of others and presents them as his or her own". (Chambers, *The Chambers Dictionary*, 1998 edition, p1250)

The SQA definition is: "failing to acknowledge sources properly and/or submitting another person's work as if it were your own". (SQA, *Coursework Authenticity: A Guide for Teachers and Lecturers*, August 2009, p1)

Examples of plagiarism include:

* purchase of an essay from the internet;

* allowing another person to carry out the work that your name is on;

* failing to accurately identify sources used;

* copying sections of text (from friends, textbooks, internet, etc.)   without acknowledging the source.

To avoid plagiarism:

* make notes from more than one source, understand the information, and then **put it into your own words**;

* acknowledge the source of all quoted material;

* read and understand the latest version of the SQA booklet 'Your Coursework' (htt p://www.sqa.org.uk/sqa/71527.html) .

9.2 Project marking

Your project amounts to one third of your final mark and is marked out of 40.

The 40 initial marks are allocated specifically to six aspects as follows:

1. Introduction (4);

2. Analysis and evaluation (12);

3. Conclusions (6);

4. Research (6);

5. Structure and coherence (8);

6. Presentation and referencing (4).

You may notice that research is only allocated 6 marks, but the quality of your research will impact greatly on the rest of your project. Your research is the foundation of a good project and if your research is inadequate your project will not impress. The computing phrase, "garbage in garbage out" describes how poor research will lead you to erroneous conclusions.

Markers are instructed to award 5 or 6 marks to research that strongly supports the economic case being put forward. The term "strongly" in the previous sentence is replaced with "sufficiently" for the award of 3 or 4 marks. Where research evidently has taken place but is of little relevance to the case put forward then 1 or 2 marks would be the award. A failure to reference your research sources or the research being irrelevant or out-of-date would result in zero marks for research. This would also impact on marks elsewhere on the project which would be built without foundations.

9.3   Project introduction

Your project introduction should:

- state the aims of your project;

- identify clearly the economic issue;

- clarify and explain its significance to the wider economy.

You begin by stating clearly the "terms of reference" for your project. Clear aims will be awarded 2 marks, but, for additional credit, you should expand and develop your aims to explain why your topic is a significant economic issue.

Your project should progress in a logical way with a coherent structure that leads naturally to your conclusions. You should include headings and subheadings that will assist the marker in following your line of reasoning. Ensure that any economic terms you use are accurate and properly explained.

Project introduction

The following text is an example of a project introduction.

Go online

"The Barnett Formula is a topical economic issue because its existence is currently being questioned. It provides for public expenditure made in England to be available to Scotland (and Wales and Northern Ireland) and enhances the amount available per person to these areas. This is often said to reflect the additional expense of providing services in regions where population density is low, and adds to the funds available in historically more deprived areas of the UK. The principal aim of the project is to establish whether there is still justification for having a Barnett Formula."

Q3:   Outline the best parts of this introduction.

....

Q4:   Indicate what improvements could be made.

....

9.4   Project analysis and evaluation

These are your findings and this is the substantive section of your project with 12 marks at stake. Marks will be awarded for the overall quality and depth of your analysis. To gain marks you will need to:

- apply economic theory to explain your data and predict economic outcomes for individuals, firms, markets or the economy;

- assess critically the significance and quality of the data your research has provided;

- decide on which factors can be given most weight and justify these decisions;

- show an understanding of the limits of economic analysis, when applied to the real world;

- show awareness of alternative economic theories and explain alternative interpretations of the data if there are any.

Mistakes to be avoided include:

- only describing and failing to explain or analyse;

- wandering away from the stated aims into remarks that are irrelevant to the terms of reference that you established;

- missing opportunities to provide relevant graphs and tables that assist your analysis.

Project analysis and evaluation

The following text is a snippet from a project analysis.

Go online

"The Barnett Formula is a 1970s device that was itself an updated from the 1880s Goschen Formula.

When additional money is allocated to spending in England, then Scotland, Wales and Northern Ireland receive a share of that additional spending provided.

There is no requirement for the devolved ministries to spend this money in a particular way that mimics English spending.

Barnett should become less and less important. The new Scotland Bill, if passed, transfers income tax raising powers to Scotland. This means the Barnett Formula will be less significant.

If you believe it is outrageous for tax income produced in one part of the country to be spent across the whole of the UK then remember that North Sea oil and gas receipts - 90% of which come from Scottish waters - are shared across the country for the benefit of all. Revenue from Scottish oil has for three decades matched approximately the additional public spending per person in Scotland."

Q5: Outline the best parts of this analysis.

....

Q6: Indicate what improvements could be made.

....

9.5   Project conclusion

Your project conclusions:

- must avoid repetition of the earlier contents of the project;
- should be consistent with the aims stated at the start of the project;
- should follow naturally from your evaluation of the research data;
- might not be straightforward and may use probabilities and judgements based on the evidence.

Mistakes that are to be avoided include:

- your conclusions not matching up with the aims of the project which you set out at the start;
- your conclusions not following logically from your findings and analysis;
- repeating earlier analysis (marks are not generally given for saying the same thing twice so your conclusions should be worded in a summative way).

Project conclusion

The following text is an example of a single conclusion.

Go online

"If the Barnett Formula were discontinued, a mechanism to redistribute from more prosperous regions to less prosperous ones would still be required within a single nation state. An effective regional policy would have to be created in its place. Pockets of deprivation across the country would continue to receive additional resources. Areas of Glasgow and some other Scottish cities rank among the most deprived and therefore whatever scheme replaced Barnett would still see the transfer of additional public spending to these areas. It might however see some redistribution to areas such as north-east England where there is some of the highest unemployment."

Q7: Outline the best parts of this single conclusion.

....

Q8: Indicate what checks should be made on a conclusion.

....

9.6   Project structure and coherence

Your project structure should be set out in the following order:

1. Start with a front cover that includes your name, the title, and the word count.

2. Include a contents page, and check the final section numbering as it may alter as you progress.

3. Write an introduction outlining clearly the issue and the range of your project, justifying your choice of topic as current and economically significant. You will also refer to the research methods you will be using.

4. Write the main body of the project, divided by headings and, if required, subheadings.

5. Follow this with your conclusions based on the research in the previous section.

6. Include a bibliography.

7. Add any appendices (up to a maximum of three). Where possible, place diagrams next to the relevant text within the main body rather than as an appendix.

Project structure and coherence

Place the following words in the appropriate sentences below:

Go online

- bibliography;

- conclusions;

- count;

- diagrams;

- economic;

- numbering;

- subheadings;

- three.

Q9: The front cover should indicate the word ....

....

Q10: After redrafting you will need to review the page .... on the contents page.

....

Q11: Your introduction should clearly justify your topic as both current and ....

....

Q12: Divide up the project with headings and ....

....

Q13: Your research will lead you directly to your ....

....

Q14: Note down your sources in a ....

....

Q15: Alongside relevant text place ....

....

Q16: The maximum number of appendices is ....

....

9.7   Project referencing and presentation

When referencing, the details to include, in brackets, following the quoted text are:

1. the title of the text or source material;

2. the name of the author (or editor);

3. the date of publishing or reprint;

4. the page number.

An example of a reference would be:

Chambers, *The Chambers Dictionary*, 1998 edition, p1250

As web sources are often updated frequently you must include the last date of access. For example the following quotation:

"an act or instance of using or closely imitating the language and thoughts of another author without authorization and the representation of that author's work as one's own."

would have the following website reference:

Dictionary.com (2015) *Plagiarism*[online], available from http://dictionary.reference. com/browse/plagiarism (accessed 13/12/15)

Here are some guidelines and good practice for presentation in your project:

* use a clear font/font size - e.g. Times New Roman, minimum point size is 12;

* double-line spacing makes it far easier on the reader (although one and a half line spacing may be an acceptable compromise between readability and economy of resources);

* margins of 25 mm (one inch) are appropriate;

* select helpful page breaks;

* number pages clearly and after edits and check they are as listed in the contents section;

* give full details of sources for any quotations or diagrams and complete a bibliography;

* place diagrams alongside relevant text.

9.8   Project bibliography

Keep a note as you go along of every relevant text and website that you read. These can be placed in alphabetical order (by author/editor/website title).

The bibliography goes at the end of your submission, for example: Heriot-Watt University, *Scholar Study Guide CfE Advanced Higher Business Management, Unit 3* (2015); Hamilton, A. In this example I have decided that the editing organisation leads rather than the author - but it could just as well have led with the author's name.

Bibliography

Q17: A check or judgement on truth or accuracy

Go online

a) Bibliography
b) Plagiarism
c) Referencing
d) Verification

. . . .

Q18: A list of items referred to in the course of writing your project

a) Bibliography
b) Plagiarism
c) Referencing
d) Verification

. . . .

Q19: Acknowledging the source of quoted material

a) Bibliography
b) Plagiarism
c) Referencing
d) Verification

. . . .

Q20: Presenting another's writing as your own

a) Bibliography
b) Plagiarism
c) Referencing
d) Verification

. . . .

9.9   Key points to consider when researching and writing your project

In summary, the key points to consider when researching and writing your project are:

- select a current issue that interests you and phrase it as a question;

- time management is important, so agree deadlines for the completion of sections of the task with your teacher and stick closely to them;

- research widely and maintain a bibliography. Watch out for developments that occur as you are writing as they may require changes to be made;

- refer closely to the way in which marks are allocated and present your project in a format that seeks to gather in these marks;

- follow the teacher's advice on layout and presentation;

- use economic theory to explain wherever possible;

- draw your conclusions from the evidence and explicitly state how the evidence leads you to your conclusions.

9.10 Summary

Summary

You should now be able to:

- develop independent research skills;

- understand the difference between qualitative and quantitative research;

- evaluate if the range of sources used is appropriate for the needs of the research;

- keep an accurate record of the research process and sources used;

- use a referencing system and bibliography and explain the importance of them.

9.11   End of topic test

End of Topic 2 test

Go online

Q21: What does your project start with?

a) A front cover
b) A contents page
c) The introduction

....

Q22: Which of the following is a suitable font and font size?

a) Times New Roman, 10
b) Tahoma, 18
c) Arial, 12

....

Q23: Primary research might involve you in:

a) producing a questionnaire.
b) surfing the internet.
c) reading a newspaper.

....

Q24: An acceptable line spacing would be:

a) single.
b) double.
c) triple.

....

Place the following words in the appropriate sentences below:

- bibliography;

- conclusions;

- diagrams;

- time;

- up-to-date;

- word count.

Q25: .... management is important.

....

Q26: Research widely and maintain a ....

....

Q27: Make sure the information is ....

....

Q28: Start with a front cover that includes your name, the title, and the ....

....

Q29: Place .... alongside relevant text.

....

Q30: Draw your .... from the evidence.

....

....

Topic 10

End of Unit 3 test

Go online

End of Unit 3 test

For the following questions, choose all the answers that apply.

Q1: Your project will require:

a) good time management.

b) wide research that you record.

c) a descriptive approach.

d) frequent repetition of your analysis.

. . . .

Q2: The project:

a) is worth a quarter of the total marks for this course.

b) must be on a topical economic issue.

c) should always include a questionnaire or survey.

d) should not exceed 4,000 words.

. . . .

Q3: Your conclusions must:

a) include a bibliography.

b) follow logically from your findings and analysis.

c) match up with the aims set out at the start of the project.

d) avoid the detailed repetition of material presented earlier in the project.

. . . .

Q4: Which of the following is neither required nor recommended?

a) Maintaining a bibliography

b) Noting the word count

c) Adding a graphic to the front cover

d) Placing diagrams alongside relevant text

. . . .

Q5: Primary, qualitative research could involve:

a) interviewing individuals for your research and recording what they say.

b) going online to find any previous research that is relevant to you project.

c) issuing a questionnaire and tallying up the scores from the ticked boxes.

d) going to a library and looking at copies of old newspapers.

. . . .

Q6: Analysing and evaluating your research will require:

a) assessing the source for reliability and possible bias.

b) ensuring that equal weight is attached to all aspects of your research.

c) the application of economic theory to the data.

d) occasionally wandering away from the stated aims to explore other areas.

. . . .

Q7: Mistakes to be avoided in your project include:

a) missing opportunities to provide relevant graphs and tables.

b) having the word count displayed on the front cover.

c) producing a project that is merely descriptive.

d) placing diagrams alongside relevant text.

. . . .

Q8: Which of the following subject titles would make the basis for a suitable project?

a) The Great Depression

b) Should the UK seek to balance its budget?

c) Why did house prices fall in 2008?

d) The meaning of globalisation

. . . .

Glossary

Bibliography

a list of works (or sources) referred to in the process of writing your dissertation

Common Agricultural Policy

an expensive system of subsidies paid to European Union farmers

Convergence

the need for an economy joining the single currency to match up with the economic indicators of existing eurozone members before joining

Deregulation

the process by which government controls on private enterprise are reduced and the free market is advanced

Developing economy

a nation with low GDP per capita and low levels for literacy and life expectancy

Economically inactive

not in the working population; neither in a job nor looking for one

Emerging economy

a nation going through a process of industrialisation and rapid growth which shares some of the features of an advanced economy, but is not yet an advanced economy

Enlargement

the widening of the European Union to include new members

Euro

the single currency used by those EU members who have joined the eurozone

Eurozone

the name given to the group of EU countries that have adopted the euro as their currency

Futures market

contract prices for the delivery and payment at some point in the future. These contracts can be traded, and the initial party to the contract may not be the one taking delivery. Certainty over future prices reduces risk and encourages companies to be involved on the futures market

Globalisation

in Economics, it refers to increases in international trade, communications and investment leading to further economic integration and the increasingly free movement of goods, capital and labour in a global marketplace

Life expectancy

the average number of years lived; life expectancy at birth can be considered a measure of the overall quality of life in a country

Literacy rates

the percentage of a population that can read and write at a given age; low levels of education hold back economic development

Multinational

firms that have production units based in more than one country

OPEC (Organisation of the Petroleum Exporting Countries)

a group of major oil producers including Saudi Arabia, who act like a cartel and meet regularly to discuss production levels and prices. Norway, the UK and the USA are among oil producers who are not members

Price transparency

comparisons of prices in different countries are made easier for consumers through the use of a single currency

Primary research

new field research designed and carried out specifically for your project

Public sector net borrowing

a measure of annual borrowing by government

Qualitative research

research that gives rise to subjective data such as opinions that can not easily be measured or aggregated

Quantitative research

research that gathers information in such a way that it may be measured and aggregated, often resulting in tables, graphs and predictions

Real GDP growth

an actual increase in the goods and services produced by a nation in a year (after allowing for the effects of inflation on prices)

Seasonally adjusted

statistics smoothed to remove regular annual changes that can cover up the overall trend, e.g. the temporary impact of school leavers in the summer on employment figures

Secondary research

desk research using material that has already been gathered for another (probably similar) purpose

Single market

a new programme of policies adopted by the EU on 1 January 1993 which advanced beyond the mere abolition of trade barriers

Spot market

the price for immediate delivery of, and payment for, a commodity, e.g. oil. The spot market is sometimes called the "cash market"

Structural deficit

the level of the deficit exists when the economy is at full employment (not in recession), arising from infrastructure spending by government

Hints for activities

Topic 8: How to organise your project (Unit 3)

Selecting a topic

Hint 1:

- *The financial crisis of 2007-08 - should the banks have been saved?* This is now out of date.

- *Should the budget deficit be reduced as quickly as planned?* This is a good question and current for a few years beyond 2016.

- *The advantages and disadvantages of joining the euro.* This title should be reworded as a question or issue.

- *Should the UK join the euro?* This is a current topic while the UK is not in the eurozone (which may be forever).

- *Why did house prices fall in 2008?* This is now out of date.

- *What were the causes of the Great Depression?* This is out of date as this is economic history.

- *What should be the favoured currency option if Scotland gained independence?* This is a good question, but check if it is acceptable given that a second referendum may never happen.

Answers to questions and activities

1 Recent trends in the national economy (Unit 2)

GDP (page 2)

Q1: A guide answer for this question is not included as it will quickly become out of date.

Q2: A guide answer for this question is not included as it will quickly become out of date.

Inflation (page 3)

Q3: A guide answer for this question is not included as it will quickly become out of date.

Q4: A guide answer for this question is not included as it will quickly become out of date.

Unemployment trends (page 4)

Q5: The economy has returned to growth and is creating jobs during the business up-turn. Measures have been put in place to make it harder to claim benefits, and many benefits have fallen behind inflation. Wage growth has remained low (and often negative in real terms). Many workers gain employment on zero-hours contracts. Employers are therefore willing to hire labour as wage inflation is not a problem and business is improving. They are also able to remain flexible with their use of labour, due to zero-hours contracts.

Q6: The rise in employment rates must be linked to recent economic growth. It may also be due partly to the reduced level of benefits.

Q7: Three noteworthy transfers of public sector companies to the private sector contributed greatly to the trend. It has also been a period of job reduction in the public sector generally. For example, councils in England have shed a significant number of jobs over this period. The aim of reducing the budget deficit has been one cause, but it could also be partly motivated by the political persuasion of the governing party.

Q8: Real earnings were falling over several years. This reflects the lack of bargaining power of trade unions and individual workers in a deep recession. Job security became the primary concern, not increased earnings.

Q9: Economic inactivity will fall due to people joining the labour market. This is probably due to long-term social changes. Historically a main component would be the increasing number of married women in the labour force. Recent changes might be the result of improved state-provided child care, or an increase in the retirement age. Recent immigrants have a remarkably high participation in the labour market and that would also reduce the overall percentage inactive. Attempts by government to encourage some with disabilities back into work may also be a factor.

Q10: A guide answer for this question is not included as it will quickly become out of date.

Q11: A guide answer for this question is not included as it will quickly become out of date.

The budget deficit (page 8)

Q12: If the budget were always to be balanced, the government would not be using budget deficits and surpluses to influence the economy. This author would be against balanced budgets as it gives up an economic lever. The metaphor might be that you take a useful club (or tool for economic management) out of your golf bag (economic policy options).

Fiscal policy is an important tool of economic management and even after the elimination of a "structural deficit", it will still be useful to run a budget deficit or surplus to assist in achieving economic aims. The deficit should be measured against GDP, and its significance is reducing as it becomes a smaller proportion of GDP.

The level of interest rates paid on government borrowing (exceptionally low in recent years) is also important when assessing the impact of the deficit.

The exchange rate (page 8)

Q13: The US dollar.

Q14: A guide answer for this question is not included as it will quickly become out of date.

Q15: A guide answer for this question is not included as it will quickly become out of date.

The balance of payments (page 9)

Q16: The value of the pound has increased 10% against the euro since the beginning of the year. This held back the UK's exports in the first three months of the year, which were down £2.7bn on the previous quarter.

Q17: A guide answer for this question is not included as it will quickly become out of date.

Q18: A guide answer for this question is not included as it will quickly become out of date.

House prices (page 10)

Q19: A guide answer for this question is not included as it will quickly become out of date.

Q20: A guide answer for this question is not included as it will quickly become out of date.

Oil prices (page 11)

Q21: Demand factors: the coldness of a northern winter; the development of substitutes; more efficient cars; changing pollution laws; boom or recession.

Supply factors: political instability; supply decisions by OPEC cartel; major incidents such as refinery fires; the short term limits of storage containers.

Q22: A guide answer for this question is not included as it will quickly become out of date.

Q23: A guide answer for this question is not included as it will quickly become out of date.

2 Controlling the budget deficit and the national debt (Unit 2)

Budget deficit reasons (page 14)

Q1: c) Recession

Q2: b) The structural deficit

Q3: a) Fiscal policy

Q4: d) Interest payments

Government borrowing (page 15)

Q5: During recessions, government spending in areas such as welfare increase but at the same time tax revenues reduce because personal and corporate incomes fall. Government also borrows for infrastructure projects and to increase spending in areas such as the NHS.

Sale of public sector assets (page 16)

Q6: In the case of Royal Mail, taking on the pension fund gave government a windfall for one year. However in the longer term, considerable liabilities for future pensions will have to be met. This means the overall effect on the public finances is unlikely to be beneficial. Assets could generate income for many years ahead if retained and run efficiently.

National debt comparison (page 17)

Q7: Belgium, Cyprus, France, Greece, Ireland, Italy, Portugal, Spain.

Q8: No solution is available as this will change over time.

Q9: No solution is available as this will change over time.

Q10: No solution is available as this will change over time.

Recent trends in UK government borrowing (page 19)

Q11: Borrowing increased from 2000 onwards peaking in 2009-10 at over £150 billion in the aftermath of the banking collapse and with the public ownership of several rescued banks. Since then it has declined gradually to under £90 billion.

Budget deficit forecast figures (page 20)

Q12: No solution is available as this will change over time.

Reliability of sources (page 21)

Q13: Sources quoted come from opposition political figures and cannot be regarded as neutral. Even if the figures produced by politicians are accurate, they may well have been selectively chosen to promote the argument that they are making. Therefore a researcher should seek to check these figures against other sources.

City analysts pointed out that income tax receipts were weak and have made deficit forecasts hard to reach.

Despite a drop in unemployment, income tax receipts are low because so many of the jobs created are low wage jobs.

End of Topic 2 test (page 22)

Q14: b) Higher rates of economic growth

Q15: b) 2009-10

Q16: c) long-term investment in infrastructure by government.

Q17: d) led to falls in UK net borrowing as a percentage of GDP.

3 Trends in the Scottish oil industry (Unit 2)

Licensing round (page 24)

Q1: The Oil and Gas authority awarded 41 new licences for oil and gas operations in the North Sea, bringing the latest licensing round to a total of 175 licences covering 353 blocks. (Source: the Press and Journal, 28 July 2015). Your answer will depend on future announcements.

Reliability of sources (page 24)

Q2: Both these predictions cover a wide range of outcomes, highlighting the difficulties in making an accurate estimate. Oil and Gas UK is an industry body so should be well-informed. The DECC is a government body, and although government statistics seemed sacrosanct a couple of decades ago, there can now be legitimate concern that they are politically tainted when not dealing with outright fact. A projection of future oil production gives a lot of scope for slanting in the preferred direction.

Quarterly output in the oil and gas sector (page 25)

Q3: The article you find should be checked for a recent date.

Brent Crude (page 26)

Q4: This varies and an up-to-date figure will be on the BBC website and many trading websites.

Market factors (page 27)

Q5:

Supply	Demand
Libya described as a "failed state"	Cold winter in the northern hemisphere
Soaring shale oil production in USA	Increasing miles per gallon of modern cars
	Reduced economic growth in China

North Sea job loss announcements (page 28)

Q6: There have been many such announcements in late 2014 and during 2015.

Q7: Each job loss reduces the spending power of an individual and their family, creating a negative multiplier in the communities in which they live. This will probably impact disproportionately on North East Scotland affecting local shopkeepers, but many purchases originate from outside this community so the effect will dissipate.

A competing positive multiplier as less is spent filling petrol tanks (and spent on more goods and services instead) may result in an outcome that is positive for the UK economy as a whole. Both effects may well be swamped (concealed) by other variables in the economic environment.

End of Topic 3 test (page 30)

Q8:   b) between $100 and $120.

Q9:   d) over 90%.

Q10:   c) economic growth around the world.

Q11:   a) new technology for developing shale oil.

Q12:   d) all of the above

4 Global economic issues: globalisation (Unit 2)

Globalisation definition (page 33)

Q1: The four basic aspects of globalisation identified by the IMF were:

- trade and transactions;
- capital and investment movements;
- migration and movement of people;
- the dissemination of knowledge.

Tata group (page 34)

Q2: The Tata group are an Indian multinational, conglomerate headquartered in Mumbai, India. They operate in the following business sectors: communications and information technology, engineering, materials, services, energy, consumer products, chemicals and core sciences. The Tata group have operations in more than 100 countries across six continents.

Major Tata companies include Tata Steel, Tata Motors, Tata Consultancy Services, Tata Power, Tata Chemicals, Tata Global Beverages, Tata Teleservices, Titan Industries, Tata Communications and Indian Hotels. Market capitalisation of all the 30 listed Tata companies is around $134 billion (as of March 2015). Approximately 70% of Tata revenue comes from outside India (figures from 2014-15).

Benefits of globalisation - video (page 35)

Q3: Norberg outlines the experience of Taiwan from the 1960s.

Taiwan adopted a deregulated market economy. Peasant farmers were given property rights and the ownership of land.

To begin with its selling points were low wages and long hours. It became well-known for producing low-technology plastic toys.

Working conditions in factories were poor by western standards, but economic growth and standards of living improved rapidly. The workers became more prosperous than they could have in the agricultural economy.

Foreign investment was attracted. There was investment in education. Skills, productivity and wages increased. Taiwan now has a technologically advanced economy. It was stated that Taiwan is 20 times richer than Kenya, a nation that was comparable just 50 years earlier.

Norberg expands his argument using the more recent example of Vietnam. He offers evidence that multinationals such as Nike have contributed to rising standards of living, and that far from damaging local enterprise, they have created a multiplier effect that extends into the wider community. A local entrepreneur is shown learning best practice from his multinational neighbour. Pay rates at Nike are much better than the local average income and, while Nike may eventually move on, they will have contributed to long-term benefits and economic advances.

By contrast, Kenya has not freed up its markets and given private enterprise its head. Land is owned by government, and regulations and costly trading licenses have restrained entrepreneurship. They are further handicapped by the international tariffs that globalisation seeks to reduce.

Benefits of globalisation (page 36)

Q4: Benefits of globalisation:

1. Improvements in standards of *living*
2. Improvements in *life* expectancy
3. Improvements in *literacy* rates
4. Dramatic reductions in *costs of production*
5. The spread of new *technology*
6. Improved *environmental* performance
7. Improvements in working *conditions*
8. Greater knowledge of and respect for other *cultures*
9. Extension of *democracy*
10. Increased *international* cooperation

Life expectancy (page 36)

Q5: The following figures are from Spring 2015:

a) UK 80, Japan 84, Canada 82;
b) Singapore 84, Taiwan 80, Brazil 73;
c) Vietnam 73;
d) Kenya 64.

As these figures are regularly updated, your answers may vary.

Note that you may not be entirely satisfied with the examples selected. Life expectancies have been affected unevenly by the spread of disease, e.g. HIV infection, and this can make the figures difficult to analyse and may cause doubts about the significance of globalisation in increasing life expectancy. It is also the case that the spread of disease is sometimes put down as a disadvantage of globalisation.

Consider carrying out your own further research into life expectancy and related figures such as infant mortality in countries at different stages of economic development and form your own considered conclusions.

Literacy rates (page 37)

Q6: The following figures are from Spring 2015:

a) Singapore 97%, Taiwan 98%, Brazil 93%;

b) Vietnam 94%;

c) Kenya 78%.

As these figures are regularly updated, your answers may vary.

Note that advanced economies such as the UK, Japan and Canada have literacy rates of 99% plus.

Effect of globalisation on the Taiwan, Brazil and Singapore economies (page 37)

Q7: There is no one solution, but any findings, for example on the CIA World Factbook (http://1.usa.gov/1FY6ErF) , on levels of economic growth, improvements in life expectancy, literacy rates, etc. are relevant.

Globalisation advantages and disadvantages (page 38)

Q8:

Advantages	Disadvantages
Dramatic reductions in costs of production	Destruction of traditional agricultural communities
Extension of democracy	Easier spread of disease
Greater knowledge of and respect for other cultures	Environmental damage
Improved environmental performance	Exploitation of workers
Improvements in life expectancy	Movement of skilled workers to richest countries
Improvements in literacy rates	Problems associated with the restructuring of economies
Improvements in standards of living	Recessions may become global
Improvements in working conditions	Unskilled workers in advanced economies face competition
Increased international cooperation	Use of child labour
The spread of new technology	Widening gap between richest and poorest countries

China's economy (page 40)

Q9: Low wages for manufacturing

Q10: In 2014 economic growth was 7%. This would exceed population growth lead to a rise in real incomes per head.

India's economy (page 40)

Q11: Your answer should look at:

* economic growth rates and standards of living;
* the changing pattern of employment (the percentages employed in primary/secondary/tertiary sectors over time);
* examples of the presence of multinational companies;
* the expansion of Indian based multinationals such as Tata;
* the changes in the Indian economy over the last few decades.

End of Topic 4 test (page 42)

Q12: c) a reduction in global warming.

Q13: b) labour mobility.

Q14: d) all of the above.

Q15: Among the responses you may include:

* evidence of manufacturing and call centre jobs being outsourced by UK companies;
* the presence of new brands on UK high streets and supermarkets;
* the extent that the migration of workers in and out of the UK has increased;
* the effect on the UK labour market and wages of the free movement of labour in the EU;
* an analysis of the causes of the UK's low inflation during the economic expansion between 1992 and 2007;
* examples of investment by foreign multinationals in the UK and examples of companies leaving the UK;
* the deregulation of the City of London in the "Big Bang" and the growth of London as an international financial centre;
* the impact on major parts of the Scottish economy (e.g. financial sector, whisky industry, seasonal agricultural employment).

5 Global economic issues: the European Union (Unit 2)

Expansion of the EU (page 44)

Expected answer

Q1: Belgium, France, Italy, Luxembourg, Netherlands, West Germany, Ireland, Portugal, Spain, Austria and Finland.

Q2: Greece (2001), Slovenia (2007), Cyprus, Malta (both 2008), Slovakia (2009), Estonia (2011), Latvia (2014) and Lithuania (2015).

Single currency options (page 47)

Q3: A suitable article for research would be the following article on the Best Thinking website - http://bit.ly/1GlMWxc

Q4: I found several useful articles on the subject, for example:

*   New Statesman website (http://bit.ly/1RjDNpp)
*   Fortune website (http://for.tn/1MykDsk)

Advantages and disadvantages of joining the eurozone (page 48)

Q5:

Advantages	Disadvantages
Easier for consumers to compare prices in different countries	Devaluation of national currency no longer possible
Exchange rate certainty for firms within eurozone	Fiscal policy subject to strict rules that limit ability to borrow in recession
Multinational investment more likely	One interest rate set for all of eurozone
No commission on changing currency	Unexpected events may lead to eurozone economies diverging

EU enlargement (page 51)

Q6: For the UK the process of enlargement has several benefits. Consumers will have a greater *choice* of products. This increases *competition* which drives down *prices*, leads to innovative behaviour by firms, and can improve the *quality* of products. Enlargement allows labour shortages to be met with *foreign workers* and keeps down wage inflation. It provides opportunities for UK based firms to improve *profitability* by moving to the lower wage economies of the new members.

Enlargement can create problems. UK workers will face more competition in the labour market and their *wages* are less likely to rise. Regional aid and CAP *subsidies* for the economic development of the new members may be expensive. Firms may move **manufacturing** and some service jobs to the new member countries to take advantage of lower wages and this will lead to some **job losses** in the UK.

Turkey - EU membership (page 52)

Q7: Benefits include that:

- it is a populous nation, that with a market economy and globalisation, has the potential to be a significant economic power;
- it provides links to energy sources to the East;
- for existing EU members, it greatly expands the single market and embraces globalisation;
- politically, the EU acting as one, would be an even more powerful block;
- culturally and politically, it provides a bridge to the Muslim world;
- it would provide a wider variety of goods for EU consumers, and be an alternative location for EU businesses to grow in.

Q8: Further progress is required on:

- women's rights;
- anti-corruption measures;
- judicial reform;
- agricultural reform;
- freedom of expression and the rights of minority religious groups.

Turkey also does not recognise Cyprus and this means it cannot open its ports and airports to all EU member states.

Turkey's current economic performance (page 52)

Q9: The solution to this would need regular updating, but you can expect to find wide disparities in areas such as GDP per capita for some time to come.

End of topic 5 test (page 55)

Q10: c) Croatia

Q11: d) 28

Q12: a) Italy

Q13: c) Romania and Bulgaria

Q14: b) Common Agricultural Policy

Q15: d) the widening of the EU by allowing in new member nations.

Q16: b) Portugal

Q17: b) the death penalty still exists in Turkey, and c) further progress is required on women's rights.

Q18: c) easily compare UK prices with those of other eurozone nations.

6 Economic growth in developing and emerging economies (Unit 2)

World factbook - emerging economies (page 58)

Q1:   No solution is available as GDP per capita and list of emerging economies will change over time.

World factbook - developing economies (page 59)

Q2:   No solution is available as GDP per capita and list of developing economies will change over time.

Factors that delay economic growth (page 60)

Q3:

Land	Labour	Capital	Enterprise
low rainfall	poor health	inadequate roads	bureaucratic "red tape"
few natural resources	limited skills	little savings	few business skills

Economic growth of developing and emerging economies (page 61)

Q4:   The figures will change every year so there is no definitive answer.

Economic growth of developing and emerging economies (page 62)

Q5:   Education, sanitation and political stability

Q6:   Any three of the following:

- high levels of private investment in business - much of it from foreign multinationals;
- high levels of investment by government in major infrastructure projects such as improvements to transport links;
- an economy rapidly diversifying into manufacturing;
- moves towards free trade and internationally open markets;
- the encouragement of entrepreneurship and a preference for free market solutions over state intervention;
- relaxed labour laws (workers are poorly protected from exploitation) and very competitive hourly wage rates.

Zambia's problems (page 63)

Q7:   Zambia's problems include:

* dependency on the world market price of copper;
* Zambia is landlocked;
* resources have been mismanaged;
* corruption, associated with one-party rule until the 1990s;
* a high level of debt;
* disease (e.g. Malaria and Aids/HIV) - the adult prevalence rate of Aids/HIV is estimated at 15%;
* hosting refugees from civil wars in neighbouring Congo and Angola;
* failure to diversify the economy which is unattractive to foreign investment;
* poverty - millions of Zambians earn less than a dollar a day;
* air pollution and acid rain in the copper/cobalt mining/refining area;
* chemical pollution of water sources;
* lack of adequate water treatment;
* poaching of animal population;
* deforestation and resulting soil erosion.

Highly Indebted Poor Country (HIPC) Initiative (page 63)

Q8:   To qualify, countries must have a level of debt that they cannot manage and must put into place structural reforms to their economy suggested by the IMF. It would be worthwhile reading some of the detailed information available on the web, for example at the IMF website (http://www.imf.org).

It provides debt relief and low interest loans to cancel or reduce external debt repayments to sustainable levels, meaning they can repay debts in a timely fashion in the future.

The price of copper (page 63)

Q9:   I located the five year spot price of copper at the Kitko website (http://www.kitco.com/).

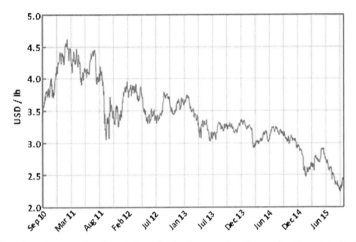

The price of copper has largely been in decline over the 5 years to 2015. Zambia is keen to diversify.

Another developing economy (page 63)

Q10: The solution will depend on your choice of country, so it is not possible to give a definitive solution.

The effect of rising oil prices on developing countries (page 65)

Q11: For your solution, extract the key points in the section above and add some research of your own. Make sure you acknowledge that some of the world's poorest countries actually have oil, and if they could manage this wealth in a wiser and less corrupt manner they make substantial improvements to education, infrastructure and living standards. For the majority of poor countries, rising oil prices will further strain their economies.

End of Topic 6 test (page 66)

Q12:

Brazil	Chad	*China*	*India*	Ireland
Italy	Malawi	Mali	*Nigeria*	*Russia*

Q13: b) levels of literacy and numeracy

Q14: c) sanitation

Q15: a) primary

Q16: The characteristics of emerging economies include:

- high levels of private investment in business - much of it from foreign multinationals;
- high levels of investment by government in major infrastructure projects such as improvements to transport links;
- an economy rapidly diversifying into manufacturing;
- moves towards free trade and internationally open markets;
- the encouragement of entrepreneurship and a preference for free market solutions over state intervention;
- relaxed labour laws (workers are poorly protected from exploitation) and very competitive hourly wage rates.

7 End of Unit 2 test

End of Unit 2 test (page 68)

Q1: c) long-term investment in infrastructure by government.

Q2: c) economic growth around the world.

Q3: d) all of the above

Q4: b) labour mobility.

Q5: d) all of the above.

Q6: d) they cannot match German levels of productivity.

Q7: c) set its own interest rates independently.

Q8: a) I) and II) only

Q9: d) I), II) and III)

Q10: b) Malawi, Brazil, Canada

Q11: Cuts in tax credits reduce the incomes of low wage earners. They have a high marginal propensity to consume. Without this income, they will reduce their level of consumption. This would lead to lower spending in shops and hence to lower orders to firms and unemployment. Economic growth would slow, VAT receipts would be less, and spending on unemployment benefits could increase. This would delay the achievement of a balanced budget. Cuts affecting those with the highest marginal propensity to consume could be counter-productive.

Cuts and delays in spending on infrastructure projects, and the holding down of public sector pay, could both also work through reduced economic growth to delay the achievement of a balanced budget.

Q12: A balanced budget stops interest rates on government borrowing soaring as the debt becomes unsustainable and there is a risk of default (as in Greece). It may prevent future tax rises or even result in lower tax rates.

The reduction of taxes and the public sector may be considered an encouragement to private enterprise. This has particular appeal to those who consider the private sector driven by the profit motive to be more efficient than public provision.

8 How to organise your project (Unit 3)

Project plan (page 73)

Q1: Possible solution:

- Topic selection: *August*
- Research: *September/October*
- Structure and first draft: *November/December*
- Evaluation and redraft: *January/February*
- Final copy: *March*

Selecting a topic (page 75)

Q2: The following are good topics because they are both current and take the form of a question to be researched:

- Should the budget deficit be reduced as quickly as planned?
- Should the UK join the euro?
- What should be the favoured currency option if Scotland gained independence?

End of Topic 1 test (page 77)

Q3: b) 10%

Q4: c) 4,000

Q5: c) 33%

Q6: a) current and economically significant.

9 How to research and write your project (Unit 3)

Qualitative or quantitative research? (page 80)

Q1: **Quantitative research** is suited to expressing your findings numerically, e.g. in the form of tables and graphs. To gather information for this type of analysis, questions normally have a permitted range of answers from which the data is collated.

Qualitative research tends to provide varying responses that can offer more detail and subtle insight but are difficult to quantify. Open-ended responses and individual opinions have to be assessed and summarised.

Researchers are prone to placing more emphasis on quantitative data. Perhaps they feel confident with numbers, and the graphs look impressive and give weight to their conclusions? Do not underestimate the insight offered by the comments received through qualitative research - even though you may not get a pretty graph at the end!

A successful questionnaire (page 80)

Q2: The design of effective questionnaires is very difficult. You may be surprised by the work required to prepare a good questionnaire and collate the responses. As a result, the first principle is to keep it short and to the point.

There are many other noteworthy points which your research may advise on. For example, if respondents have to tick boxes use four options, not three or five. This will make it more difficult for the respondents to sit on the fence and cluster in the middle.

Project introduction (page 82)

Q3: The economic issue is clearly identified in the first few words. It is reasonable to claim the debate on the future of the Barnett Formula as a topical economic issue. Some clarification of the significance to the wider economy has been made.

Q4: The aims of the project are not clearly stated, and further development is required. Can the title been stated as an economic question to be investigated? It is too short to fulfill all the requirements of a good introduction

Project analysis and evaluation (page 83)

Q5: It offers a very basic beginning. We have some relevant facts (and providing they match stated aims for this project) they provide an opportunity for further development and analysis with examples and figures. For example, it begins to answer how Barnett operates; and whether Scotland is a net gainer overall on public spending per head (if these were aims). It also infers that there may be less need for it in the future, but much more detail is needed before conclusions can be reasonably drawn.

Q6: As an excerpt we cannot be too critical since we know not what the rest of the analysis showed. However this section:

a) is merely descriptive, making assertions which are not properly backed up;

b) is entirely devoid of figures. Are there no numbers (and graphs) that could be used to back up the assertions made?

c) misses an opportunity for an example such as the way in which "Barnett consequentials" for health spending in England have been used in Scotland;

d) deals with several issues quickly and should be divided into subsections for development.

Project conclusion (page 84)

Q7: This conclusion is summative.

If an aim were to consider what might replace the Barnett Formula, then this is a relevant conclusion. It could be backed up by having rates of unemployment across the UK regions (easily available) in the earlier analysis and perhaps quoting the unemployment rates in Scotland and North-East England in the conclusion.

Q8: Confirm that the conclusion:

a) matches up with a stated aim of this project;

b) derives from earlier findings and analysis;

c) is summative and does not just repeat earlier detailed analysis.

Project structure and coherence (page 85)

Q9: The front cover should indicate the word *count*.

Q10: After redrafting you will need to review the page *numbering* on the contents page.

Q11: Your introduction should clearly justify your topic as both current and *economic*.

Q12: Divide up the project with headings and *subheadings*.

Q13: Your research will lead you directly to your *conclusions*.

Q14: Note down your sources in a *bibliography*.

Q15: Alongside relevant text place *diagrams*.

Q16: The maximum number of appendices is *three*.

Bibliography (page 87)

Q17: d) Verification

Q18: a) Bibliography

Q19: c) Referencing

Q20: b) Plagiarism

End of Topic 2 test (page 90)

Q21: a) A front cover

Q22: c) Arial, 12

Q23: a) producing a questionnaire.

Q24: b) double.

Q25: *Time* management is important.

Q26: Research widely and maintain a *bibliography*.

Q27: Make sure the information is *up-to-date*.

Q28: Start with a front cover that includes your name, the title, and the *word count*.

Q29: Place *diagrams* alongside relevant text.

Q30: Draw your *conclusions* from the evidence.

10 End of Unit 3 test

End of Unit 3 test (page 94)

Q1: (a) good time management and (b) wide research that you record.

Q2: (b) must be on a topical economic issue and (c) should not exceed 4,000 words.

Q3: (b) follow logically from your findings and analysis, (c) match up with the aims set out at the start of the project and (d) avoid the detailed repetition of material presented earlier in the project.

Q4: (c) Adding a graphic to the front cover

Q5: (a) interviewing individuals for your research and recording what they say.

Q6: (a) assessing the source for reliability and possible bias and (c) the application of economic theory to the data.

Q7: (a) missing opportunities to provide relevant graphs and tables and (c) producing a project that is merely descriptive.

Q8: (b) Should the UK seek to balance its budget?